Standard Grade | General | Credit

English

Leckie×Leckie

© Scottish Qualifications Authority

First exam published in 2004.
Published by Leckie & Leckie Ltd, 3rd Floor, 4 Queen Street, Edinburgh EH2 1JE
tel: 0131 220 6831 fax: 0131 225 9987 enquiries@leckieandleckie.co.uk www.leckieandleckie.co.uk

ISBN 978-1-84372-629-6

A CIP Catalogue record for this book is available from the British Library.

Leckie & Leckie is a division of Huveaux plc.

Leckie & Leckie is grateful to the copyright holders, as credited at the back of the book, for permission to use their material.
Every effort has been made to trace the copyright holders and to obtain their permission for the use of copyright material.
Leckie & Leckie will gladly receive information enabling them to rectify any error or omission in subsequent editions.

[BLANK PAGE]

G

0860/403

| NATIONAL QUALIFICATIONS 2004 | WEDNESDAY, 5 MAY 1.00 PM – 1.50 PM | ENGLISH STANDARD GRADE General Level Reading Text |

Read carefully the passage overleaf. It will help if you read it twice. When you have done so, answer the questions. Use the spaces provided in the Question/Answer booklet.

SCOTTISH QUALIFICATIONS AUTHORITY

Pucker Way to Kiss a Hummingbird

Mark Carwardine puts on lipstick in Arizona for a wild encounter.

1   There's a rather embarrassing tradition in wildlife circles in certain parts of Arizona. Visiting naturalists are encouraged to try to "kiss" a wild hummingbird.

2   This is more of a challenge for men than it is for women – mainly because it involves wearing lots of red lipstick. A dress and high heels are optional, but the redder and thicker the lipstick the better. Hummingbirds drink nectar from flowers that are often bright red and have learned to associate this particular colour with food. They mistake your mouth for one of their favourite plants – at least, that's the theory.

3   Which is how I found myself high in the mountains of South-East Arizona, with puckered lips pointing sky-ward and a crowd of bemused onlookers egging me on.

4   My home for a couple of days was Beatty's Guest Ranch near the Mexico border. Run by Tom and Edith Beatty, the ranch is nearly 6,000ft above sea level, nestling between two enormous peaks, with spectacular views down the valley to the desert below.

5   According to the South-Eastern Arizona Bird Observatory, it is the hottest hummingbird-watching spot in the state. Thousands of "hummers" arrive in April and May and stay until early October. No fewer than 15 different species are found here on a regular basis.

6   Dozens of special hummingbird feeders, looking like upside-down jam jars, are dotted around the ranch. Hanging from trees, bushes, fences and buildings they are full of a simple magic potion (four parts water, one part white sugar) similar to the nectar of hummingbird flowers. Tom and Edith keep the feeders topped up, getting through a mind-boggling 550 2lb bags of sugar in a typical year.

7   There were two feeders outside my

SUMMER SPECTACLE:
Thousands of hummingbirds arrive in Arizona every year

bedroom window in the turn-of-the-century self-catering cabin on the forest edge (not a good place to stay if you've seen *Friday The 13th* or *The Blair Witch Project*, but idyllic in every other sense).

8   I will never forget pulling back the curtains on the first morning. There were hummingbirds everywhere, whizzing backwards and forwards past the window like demented bees. Sometimes they paused in front of the sugar-water to feed, either perching or hovering with the immaculate precision of experienced helicopter pilots.

9   Apparently, it's possible to see as many as ten species at the ranch in just half an hour. But even when they stayed still for more than a few moments I had no idea which was which. As they moved around, their colours changed in relation to the angle of the sun. Bird identification is hard enough at the best of times, but this was ridiculous.

10   Take a male hummingbird, for example. When you look at it face-to-face its throat is a fiery scarlet red. But as it turns away the colour shifts – first to orange, then yellow, then blackish-brown and then green. Try identifying that in a hurry, before it turns

into a blur and helicopters away.

11   I think there were Anna's hummingbirds, black-chinned, broad billed, blue-throated, magnificent, red and violet-crowned that morning, but I'm not entirely sure. Later, I asked other bird-watchers about similar-looking hummers around "their" feeding station, but they weren't sure either. I left them bickering over the difference between the sapphire blue throat of a broad-bill and the cobalt blue throat of a blue-throat.

12   The biological advantage of changing colour is that the birds can control the way they look. If a male wants to impress a female he shows his best side, but if he wants to hide from a predator he merely turns away and almost disappears among the greenery.

13   According to Sheri Williamson, hummingbird expert and co-founder of the South-Eastern Arizona Bird Observatory, you can tell them apart by the sound of their wings. Broad-tailed hummingbirds, for example, have a metallic trill to their wingbeats, while male black-chinned hummingbirds make a dull, flat whine.

14   Sheri took me to see a hummingbird in the hand. There's a ringing station, or banding station as they call it in the States, at nearby Sierra Vista. It's open to the public and every weekend the observatory staff rig up a mist-net trap with a tasty-looking sugar-water feeder in the middle. Whenever a hummingbird dares an investigatory hover, a burly member of the observatory team rushes forward, waving his arms around, and ushers the unfortunate bird inside.

15   We caught lots of hummingbirds that day. One was a female black-chinned that squealed when she was caught. It was hard to tell whether this was out of fear or anger ("How could I, so fleet of wing, be caught by this enormous fool?"). We found her abdomen distended with an enormous egg, which Sheri guessed would be laid before nightfall.

16   For a brief moment, I actually held the delicate bundle of feathers in my hand, and was so nervous about squeezing too hard that she escaped. After hovering above us for a moment, she made a bee-line for the bushes.

17   Hovering hummingbirds draw crowds of naturalists from all over the world to South-East Arizona, but hovering does have one major drawback. Pound for pound, beating your wings 70 times per second uses more energy than any other activity in the animal kingdom. Living life in the fast lane means hummingbirds need a continuous supply of fuel.

18   A typical hummingbird eats around half its own weight in energy-rich nectar every day. To do that it has to keep others away from its favourite foodplants. I spent many hours watching them battle it out at feeding stations. Far from being all sweetness and light, they are little fighter pilots. If they were the size of ravens it wouldn't be safe to walk in the woods.

19   Before I left, there was one thing I had to do. Dutifully, I put on bright red lipstick, took a mouthful of sugar-water, sat back, puckered my lips . . . and waited. Within 30 seconds two hummingbirds came to investigate. Others soon followed.

20   I sat there for an eternity not daring to move. No hummingbird actually drank sugar-water from my mouth (who can blame them?), but several did hover so close I could feel their wingbeats against my cheeks.

21   Strangely, the encounter was every bit as impressive as rubbing shoulders with mountain gorillas in the wilds of Africa or performing slow-motion underwater ballets with dolphins in the Bahamas.

22   Even better, my biggest worry came to nothing – the red lipstick wiped off.

(*Adapted from an article by Mark Carwardine*)

[*END OF PASSAGE*]

[BLANK PAGE]

FOR OFFICIAL USE

G

Total
Mark

0860/404

NATIONAL
QUALIFICATIONS
2004

WEDNESDAY, 5 MAY
1.00 PM – 1.50 PM

ENGLISH
STANDARD GRADE
General Level
Reading
Questions

Fill in these boxes and read what is printed below.

Full name of centre

Town

Forename(s)

Surname

Date of birth
Day Month Year

Scottish candidate number

Number of seat

NB Before leaving the examination room you must give this booklet to the invigilator. If you do not, you may lose all the marks for this paper.

SCOTTISH
QUALIFICATIONS
AUTHORITY

SAB 0860/404 6/71420

©

Marks

QUESTIONS

Write your answers in the spaces provided.

Look at Paragraphs 1 and 2.

1. **Write down a word** from Paragraph 1 that suggests naturalists might be reluctant to kiss a hummingbird.

   _____

   2 ■ 0

2. Why are the hummingbirds attracted to someone wearing bright red lipstick?

   _____

   _____

   2 1 0

3. Why do you think the writer uses the word "theory" in Paragraph 2?

   _____

   2 ■ 0

Look at Paragraphs 3 and 4.

4. Where **exactly** did the writer first meet the hummingbirds?

   _____

   _____

   2 1 0

Look at Paragraphs 5 and 6.

5. Thousands of "hummers" (Paragraph 5)

   Why has the writer put the word "hummers" in inverted commas?

   _____

   _____

   2 ■ 0

PAGE
TOTAL

Marks

6. "Hanging from trees, bushes, fences and buildings they are full of a simple magic potion . . . flowers." (Paragraph 6)

Identify and comment on the effect of **two features** of the structure of this sentence.

(i) _____

_____ 2 | 1 | 0

(ii) _____

_____ 2 | 1 | 0

7. **Write down an expression** from Paragraph 6 which tells you that the writer is surprised by the amount of sugar used.

_____ 2 | ■ | 0

Look at Paragraphs 7 and 8.

8. What do the expressions "whizzing" and "like demented bees" tell you about the movement of the hummingbirds?

_____

_____ 2 | 1 | 0

9. **Write down an expression** which shows that the writer admires the flying skills of the hummingbird.

_____ 2 | ■ | 0

Look at Paragraphs 9 and 10.

10. **In your own words** write down **two** reasons why the writer found bird identification "ridiculous". 2 | 1 | 0

(i) _____

(ii) _____

Page three   **[Turn over**

PAGE
TOTAL

Marks

Look at Paragraphs 11 and 12.

11. What does the writer's use of the word "bickering" tell you about his attitude to the bird watchers?

_____   2 ■ 0

12. **In your own words** give **two** reasons why hummingbirds change their colour.   2 1 0

    (i) _____

    (ii) _____

Look at Paragraphs 13 to 15.

13. How does Sheri Williamson tell the difference between hummingbirds?

    _____

    _____   2 1 0

14. Comment on the writer's use of the expression "hummingbird in the hand".

    _____

    _____   2 1 0

15. "Whenever a hummingbird dares an investigatory hover, a burly member of the observatory team rushes forward, waving his arms around" (Paragraph 14)

    How does this description create effective contrasts?

    (i) _____   2 ■ 0

    (ii) _____   2 ■ 0

Look at Paragraph 16.

16. What does the expression "I actually held" tell you about how the writer felt when he held the hummingbird?

    _____

    _____   2 ■ 0

Marks

Look at Paragraphs 17 and 18.

17. "Living life in the fast lane means hummingbirds need a continuous supply of fuel." (Paragraph 17)

Explain the effectiveness of this image.

_____

_____

_____ **2 1 0**

18. **In your own words**, what **two** new impressions does the writer give of the hummingbird in Paragraph 18?

_____

_____ **2 1 0**

Look at Paragraphs 19 to 22.

19. "Dutifully, I put on bright red lipstick . . . puckered my lips . . . and waited." (Paragraph 19)

Identify and comment on any **one feature** of structure **or** punctuation in this sentence.

_____

_____

_____ **2 1 0**

20. **Write down an expression** from Paragraph 20 which tells us the writer felt he waited for a long time.

_____ **2 ■ 0**

21. **In your own words** what does the writer's use of the word "Strangely" tell you about his reaction to the encounter with the hummingbirds?

_____

_____ **2 ■ 0**

[Turn over for Questions 22 and 23 on *Page six*

PAGE TOTAL

Marks

Think about the passage as a whole.

22. From the passage **write down an example** of the writer's use of humour.

    Explain why it is effective.

    _____

    _____

    _____   2 1 0

23. Overall how do you think the writer feels about his experience with the humming-birds?

    Support your answer by referring to the passage.

    _____

    _____

    _____   2 1 0

[END OF QUESTION PAPER]

PAGE
TOTAL

[BLANK PAGE]

C

0860/405

NATIONAL
QUALIFICATIONS
2004

WEDNESDAY, 5 MAY
2.30 PM – 3.20 PM

ENGLISH
STANDARD GRADE
Credit Level
Reading
Text

Read carefully the passage overleaf. It will help if you read it twice. When you have done so, answer the questions. Use the spaces provided in the Question/Answer booklet.

SCOTTISH
QUALIFICATIONS
AUTHORITY

©

The following extract is taken from a novel set on a Greek island during the Second World War.

1   When Pelagia entered the kitchen she stopped singing abruptly, and was seized with consternation. There was a stranger seated at the kitchen table, a most horrible and wild stranger who looked worse than the brigands of childhood tales. The man was quite motionless except for the rhythmic fluttering and trembling of his hands. His head was utterly concealed beneath a cascade of matted hair that seemed to have no form nor colour. In places it stuck out in twisted corkscrews, and in others it lay in congealed pads like felt; it was the hair of a hermit demented by solitude. Beneath it Pelagia could see nothing but an enormous and disorderly beard surmounted by two tiny bright eyes that would not look at her. There was a nose in there, stripped of its skin, reddened and flaked, and glimpses of darkened, streaked and grimy flesh.

2   The stranger wore the unidentifiable and ragged remains of a shirt and trousers, and a kind of overcoat cut out of animal skins that had been tacked together with thongs of sinew. Pelagia saw, beneath the table, that in place of shoes his feet were bound with bandages that were both caked with old, congealed blood, and the bright stains of fresh. He was breathing heavily, and the smell was inconceivably foul; it was the reek of rotting flesh, of festering wounds, of ancient perspiration, and of fear. She looked at the hands that were clasped together in the effort to prevent their quivering, and was overcome both with fright and pity. What was she to do?

3   "My father's out," she said. "He should be back tomorrow."

4   "Ice," said the stranger, as though he had not heard her, "I'll never be warm again." His voice cracked and she realised that his shoulders were heaving. "Oh, the ice," he repeated. He held his hands before his face. He wrapped his fingers together, and his whole body seemed to be fighting to suppress a succession of spasms.

5   "You can come back tomorrow," said Pelagia, appalled by this gibbering apparition, and completely at a loss.

6   "No crampons, you see. The snow is whipped away by the wind, and the ice is in ridges, sharper than knives, and when you fall you are cut. Look at my hands." He held them up to her, palm outwards in the gesture that would normally be an insult, and she saw the horrendous cross-tracking of hard white scars that had obliterated every natural line, scored away the pads and calluses, and left seeping cracks across the joints. There were no nails and no trace of cuticles.

7   "And the ice screams. It shrieks. And voices call to you out of it. And you look into it and you see people. They beckon and wave, and they mock, and you shoot into the ice but they don't shut up, and then the ice squeaks. It squeaks all night, all night."

8   "Look, you can't stay," said Pelagia.

9   Her perplexity was growing into an acute anxiety as she wondered what on earth she was supposed to do on her own with a mad vagrant ranting in her kitchen. She thought of leaving him there and running out to fetch help; but was paralysed by the thought of what he might do or steal in her absence. "Please leave," she pleaded. "My father will be back tomorrow, and he can . . . see to your feet."

10   The man responded to her for the first time, "I can't walk. No boots."

11   Psipsina entered the room and sniffed the air, her whiskers twitching as she sampled the strong and unfamiliar smells. She ran across the floor in her fluid

manner, and leapt up onto the table. She approached the neolithic man and burrowed in the remains of a pocket, emerging triumphantly with a small cube of white cheese that she demolished with evident satisfaction. She returned to the pocket and found only a broken cigarette, which she discarded.

12   The man smiled, revealing good teeth but bleeding gums, and he petted the animal about the head. "Ah, at least Psipsina remembers me," he said, and silent tears began to follow each other down his cheeks and into his beard. "She still smells sweet."

13   Pelagia was astounded. Psipsina was afraid of strangers, and how did this ghastly ruin know her name? Who could have told him? She wiped her hands on her apron for the lack of any sense of what to think or do, and said, "Mandras?"

14   The man turned his face towards her and said, "Don't touch me, Pelagia. I've got lice. I didn't know what to do, and I came here first. All the time I knew I had to get here first, that's all, and I'm tired. Do you have any coffee?"

15   Pelagia's mind became void, decentred by a babble of emotions. She felt despair, unbearable excitement, guilt, pity, revulsion. Her heart jumped in her chest and her hands fell to her side. Perhaps more than anything else, she felt helpless. It seemed inconceivable that this desolate ghost concealed the soul and body of the man she had loved and desired and missed so much, and then finally dismissed. "You never wrote to me," she said, coming up with the first thing that entered her head, the accusation that had rankled in her mind from the moment of his departure, the accusation that had grown into an angry, resentful monster.

16   Mandras looked up wearily, and said, as though it were he that pitied her, "I can't write."

17   For a reason that she did not understand, Pelagia was more repelled by this admission than by his filth. Had she betrothed herself to an illiterate, without even knowing it? For the sake of something to say she asked, "Couldn't someone else have written for you? I thought you were dead. I thought you . . . couldn't love me."

Adapted from *Captain Corelli's Mandolin* by Louis de Bernières

[END OF PASSAGE]

[BLANK PAGE]

FOR OFFICIAL USE

C

Total Mark 4

0860/406

NATIONAL
QUALIFICATIONS
2004

WEDNESDAY, 5 MAY
2.30 PM – 3.20 PM

ENGLISH
STANDARD GRADE
Credit Level
Reading
Questions

Fill in these boxes and read what is printed below.

Full name of centre

Madras College

Town

St Andrews

Forename(s)

Caitlin

Surname

Rottger

Date of birth
Day Month Year
0 7 0 7 9 4

Scottish candidate number

Number of seat

**NB Before leaving the examination room you must give this booklet to the invigilator.
If you do not, you may lose all the marks for this paper.**

SCOTTISH
QUALIFICATIONS
AUTHORITY

QUESTIONS

Write your answers in the spaces provided.

Marks

Look at Paragraph 1.

1. Quote **two** words used by the writer to convey the suddenness of Pelagia's reactions as she entered the kitchen.

(i) _abruptly_ ✓

(ii) _Seized_ ✓

2 1 0

2. Quote the expression which sums up Pelagia's impression of the stranger.

"a most horrible and wild stranger who looked worse than the brigands of childhood tales"

2 ■ 0

3. **In your own words** what contrasting image does the writer give of the movements of the man?

The man was still apart from the constant movement from his hands

2 1 0

4. What **two** ideas are suggested by the expression "a hermit demented by solitude"?

(i) It was lifeless

(ii) flat

2 1 **0**

5. Explain fully why it was difficult for Pelagia to get a clear view of the stranger's face.

Because his hair and his beard was out of control covering it.

2 1 0

Look at Paragraph 2.

6. "congealed blood, and the bright stains of fresh."

What does this description tell you about the wounds to the man's feet?

that he's got old and new wounds, he's probably been walking without shoes for a while

2 1 0

PAGE TOTAL

10

[0860/406]

Page two

12

Marks

7. "it was the reek of rotting flesh . . . fear."

Explain fully how the writer emphasises the smell from the stranger

  (i) through sentence structure.

Alliteration - reek, rotting and a metaphor

2 1 ⓪

  (ii) through word choice.

the writer uses words that give you 'an good idea what he looks like eg reek, rotting, festering perspiration

② 1 0

8. (a) **In your own words** what **two** conflicting emotions did Pelagia feel when she looked at the man?

She was scared but she was sympathetic

② 1 0

(b) Explain how the writer conveys Pelagia's dilemma.

by saying "What was she to do"

② ■ 0

Look at Paragraphs 3 to 5.

9. "My father's out," she said. "He should be back tomorrow."

What does Pelagia hope to achieve by making this statement?

She hopes that the man will leave because she thinks he's come to see her father

② ■ 0

10. Why is "gibbering" (Paragraph 5) an appropriate word to describe the stranger at this point?

because he's not making any sense "Oh, the ice"

② 1 0

[Turn over

12

9

PAGE TOTAL

Marks

Look at Paragraphs 6 and 7.

11. What **two** features of the ice disturbed the man most?   ② 1 0

(i) _that it was sharp_ ✓

(ii) _that it squeaks_

12. **Identify** any **two techniques** used by the writer in Paragraph 7 which help to convey the man's sense of panic and distress.   ② 1 0

Short sentences   Alliteration

(i) ~~Short sentences~~ ~~repetition~~ "The ice screams. It

~~Shrieks~~ (ii) _repetition — "all night, "all night_

Look at Paragraphs 8 to 10.

13. What are the options that Pelagia is considering in Paragraph 9?

She conciders leaving him in the house while

she gets help   2 ① 0

Look at Paragraphs 11 and 12.

14. Quote **two** words from Paragraph 11 which suggest that Psipsina was unhappy with her second visit to the man's pocket.   ② 1 0

(i) _only_ ✓

(ii) _discarded_ ✓

15. "Ah, at least Psipsina remembers me," (Paragraph 12)

What does this imply about the man's feelings towards Pelagia?

that he's ~~sad~~ bitter that she didn't

remember him.   ② ■ 0

9

PAGE
TOTAL

Marks

Look at Paragraphs 13 and 14.

16. "Pelagia was astounded."

How does the sentence structure in the rest of this paragraph develop Pelagia's sense of astonishment?

~~she~~ there are alot of questions which suggest she's astounded

(2) 1 0

17. "The man turned his face towards her and said, 'Don't touch me, Pelagia.'"

Why might this statement by Mandras be considered ironic?

Because he was dirty and sweaty so you wouldn't think anybody would want to touch him

(2) 1 0

Look at Paragraphs 15 to 17.

18. Tick (✓) the appropriate box to show which of the following best describes the relationship between Mandras and Pelagia.

Brother	☐	Father	☐
Husband	☐	Fiancé	✓

Justify your answer with close reference to the text.

It say that "he was the man she ~~des~~ loved, and desired" it also says "had she betrothed ~~hers~~ herself to an illiterate

(2) 1 0

19. **Identify one way** in which the writer conveys the intensity of Pelagia's feelings about the fact that Mandras had not written.

It was the first thing she said to him after she realised who he was

(2) ■ 0

[Turn over for Questions 20 to 22 on *Page six*

8

PAGE
TOTAL

Page five

Marks

20. **In your own words** explain fully how Pelagia felt when Mandras confessed he could not write.

She felt ~~more~~ apalled and ashamed than ~~he was~~ ~~the man she chose~~ she was by his dirt

② 1 0

Think about the passage as a whole.

21. How does each of the characters change in the course of the passage? **(Clear change must be indicated.)**

Pelagia Starts out as scared and pities Mandras but when she knows who he is she feels a mixture of excitement and despair

2 ① 0

Mandras Starts out ~~as a mad lunatic but then becomes~~ Seems to ~~evolve in~~ scared but then becomes more relaxed

2 1 0

22. For whom do you feel more sympathy – Pelagia or Mandras?

Justify your choice by close reference to the passage.

Pelagia because she had to wait for him not knowing whether he was dead or just simply didn't love her.

② 1 0

[END OF QUESTION PAPER]

5

PAGE TOTAL

[BLANK PAGE]

G

0860/403

NATIONAL
QUALIFICATIONS
2005

WEDNESDAY, 4 MAY
1.00 PM – 1.50 PM

ENGLISH
STANDARD GRADE
General Level
Reading
Text

Read carefully the passage overleaf. It will help if you read it twice. When you have done so, answer the questions. Use the spaces provided in the Question/Answer booklet.

SCOTTISH
QUALIFICATIONS
AUTHORITY

©

Dazzled by the Stars

Our love affair with fame may be bad for our health, according to new research. **John Harlow** reports on "celebrity worship syndrome".

1 Under her bed Katherine Hicks keeps six years of yellowing newspaper clippings about the former pop band Boyzone, and 70 videos of their performances. There might have been more if her attention had not moved on to Westlife, another pop sensation.

2 In one year she has spent £3,000 to watch Westlife perform 17 times, and is such a regular concert fan that she believes the band now recognise her as an acquaintance, if not a friend.

3 She has fixed her sights on a new star: David Sneddon, first winner of the television show Fame Academy. She cornered Sneddon at two television appearances, though it is early days in her "acquaintance" with him. Yet she felt forced to defend him indignantly against a TV presenter who, she thought, had not shown Sneddon sufficient respect.

4 Hicks is no deluded young teen: she is a 28-year-old electrical engineer. But she freely admits to an "addiction" to the latest musical sensations. "I have an obsessive nature. Anything I do is full-on, but it has never caused me problems," she said last week. "I don't do anything I cannot afford, and I don't ring in sick at work to get time off."

5 She is no stalker or obsessive; she is just "fascinated by the real personas of these people". Though she likens her behaviour to an "addiction rather than an illness", she sees nothing odd in it.

6 "Other people think I am ill or sad," she said, "but I am not missing out on anything."

7 Psychologists, who are taking an increasing interest in the effects of celebrity culture, might disagree. As Anglo-American research published last week reveals, our relationship with celebrities is more complicated than we realise. The strength of our interest in celebrities, say academics, may affect our mood.

8 Lynn McCutcheon, of DeVry University in Florida, John Maltby, of Leicester University, and two colleagues will publish a book next year exposing the psychological needs and drives behind celebrity worship.

9 But initial results of research they have conducted show that about a third of people suffer from what the researchers call "celebrity worship syndrome" and it affects their mental wellbeing.

10 It raises a troubling question: in the era of "industrialised fame", is hero worship bad for you?

11 Perhaps we should blame the start of it on Alexander the Great who, more than 2,000 years ago, exploited to the full the idea of the beautiful "god-king".

12 But if celebrity has been a cultural phenomenon for centuries, why should it have become a problem now? McCutcheon and Maltby believe the scale of it has made a huge jump in recent years. The average westerner is now exposed to hundreds of star images every day, through advertising, broadcasting, fashion, the internet and innumerable other forms.

13 Though sales of some celebrity magazines are slipping, figures show that new publications are thriving. In America, the thirst for star images is so strong that one photographer was recently paid £70,000 for a single picture.

14 David Beckham is now so famous that one paper set out on a humorous quest to find someone who did not know who he was: they finally tracked down an innocent in the Saharan city of Timbuktu.

15 The rapid growth of fan-based internet sites spreads gossip, the lifeblood of celebrity, at lightning speed. There are

more than 100,000 sites dedicated to Madonna alone.

16 Such a speedy development has prompted the academics to create the celebrity attitude scale. Using a series of questions designed to gauge personality and the level of interest in celebrities, they surveyed 700 people.

17 Most were just casually interested in stars. But one in five people displayed a determined interest. They even rearrange their social lives, for example, to follow their chosen celebrity.

18 Some 10% of people displayed such "intense-personal" attitudes towards celebrities that they showed signs of addiction.

19 It can lead to extreme actions. On both sides of the Atlantic, some fans have resorted to plastic surgery to look more like their heroes. A Scottish actor had himself turned into a Pierce Brosnan lookalike and admits he now often walks and talks like 007.

20 Dr Nicholas Chugay, a Beverly Hills surgeon, has turned various Californians into Elvis Presley or Cher. "I have had to turn some people away because I do not feel it would be good for them to let such

worship take over their lives," said Chugay.

21 BUT it may not be all that bad. Indeed, other academics argue that the likes of Beckham and Madonna are even good for you. They say that celebrity culture is based on sound reasons: by watching and imitating our so-called betters, whether it be in clothes or habits, we learn to flourish in human society.

22 Francisco Gil-White, of Pennsylvania University, argues we need celebrities to show us the road to success. He says they provide the educational and entertaining fables once sought in fairy tales.

23 "It makes sense to copy winners, because whoever is getting more of what everybody wants, and in this society this includes media attention, is probably using successful methods to get it."

24 But though some role models, such as Gareth Gates, the singer, and Tiger Woods, the golfer, can maintain they are blazing a trail for others to follow, can less worthy idols cause damage? Nancy Salzburg, who is researching charisma at San Diego University, said bad idols can cause trouble for their followers.

25 Choose well and there are benefits in celebrity, says Maltby. "It may help people to develop a relationship with and understand the world. If you admire someone like David Beckham, for example, and follow his dietary regime and the way he plays football, there can be a positive outcome in doing that."

26 Mark Griffiths, a professor of psychology at Nottingham Trent University, agrees.

27 "It was quite clear that for fans their idols formed a healthy part of their life," he said. "It was a way of raising their self-esteem.

28 What has happened is that people are not so religious and they don't look up to political and religious leaders any more. They have been replaced by the David Beckhams and the pop stars and film stars. That's who you see on the walls of teenagers' rooms because these are the people they look up to and admire."

Adapted from an article by
John Harlow

[*END OF PASSAGE*]

[BLANK PAGE]

FOR OFFICIAL USE

G

Total
Mark

0860/404

NATIONAL
QUALIFICATIONS
2005

WEDNESDAY, 4 MAY
1.00 PM – 1.50 PM

ENGLISH
STANDARD GRADE
General Level
Reading
Questions

Fill in these boxes and read what is printed below.

Full name of centre

Town

Forename(s)

Surname

Date of birth
Day Month Year

Scottish candidate number

Number of seat

NB Before leaving the examination room you must give this booklet to the invigilator. If you do not, you may lose all the marks for this paper.

SCOTTISH
QUALIFICATIONS
AUTHORITY

©

Marks

QUESTIONS

Write your answers in the spaces provided.

Look at Paragraphs 1 and 2.

1. What evidence is there to suggest that Katherine Hicks was a keen fan of Boyzone?

    _____

    _____   2   1   0

2. **Write down three key facts** which clearly show that Katherine Hicks is now a keen Westlife fan.   2   1   0

    (i)   _____

    (ii) _____

    (iii) _____

Look at Paragraph 3.

3. Why do you think the writer uses the expression "fixed her sights"?

    _____

    _____   2   ■   0

4. "early days in her "acquaintance" with him"

    Why has the writer put the word "acquaintance" in inverted commas?

    _____

    _____   2   ■   0

5. What do the words "forced" and "indignantly" in Paragraph 3 tell you about Katherine's reactions to the TV presenter's treatment of David Sneddon?

    _____   2   1   0

PAGE TOTAL

Marks

Look at Paragraphs 4 to 6.

6. "Hicks is no deluded young teen: she is a 28-year-old electrical engineer." (Paragraph 4)

   What does this statement tell you about the writer's attitude towards Katherine's behaviour?

   _____   2 ■ 0

7. (*a*) Which of the following best describes Katherine's attitude towards her "addiction"?

   Tick (✓) the appropriate box.

   Concerned   ☐

   Guilty   ☐

   Relaxed   ☐   2 ■ 0

   (*b*) **Quote an expression** to support your answer.

   _____   2 ■ 0

Look at Paragraphs 7 to 10.

8. **Give three reasons** why psychologists are showing an increasing interest in "celebrity culture".   2 1 0

   (i) _____

   (ii) _____

   (iii) _____

9. Explain why the writer ends Paragraph 10 with a question.

   _____   2 ■ 0

PAGE TOTAL

Marks

Look at Paragraphs 11 to 14.

10. Who does the writer suggest is to blame for the start of hero worship?

_____

2 ■ 0

11. Quote an expression which shows that celebrity worship is nothing new.

_____

2 ■ 0

12. In your own words explain why the scale of hero worship has made a huge jump in recent years.

_____

_____

_____

2 1 0

13. What does the word "thirst" suggest about the American attitude towards celebrity gossip?

_____

_____

2 ■ 0

14. Why do you think the writer includes the information about the quest in Paragraph 14?

_____

_____

2 1 0

Look at Paragraphs 15 to 18.

15. What has helped to spread celebrity gossip at great speed?

_____

2 ■ 0

PAGE
TOTAL

Marks

16. **In your own words** what is the "celebrity attitude scale" designed to reveal?

_____

_____ | 2 | 1 | 0

Look at Paragraphs 19 and 20.

17. In what **two** ways does the writer show the extent of celebrity "addiction"? | 2 | 1 | 0

(i) _____

(ii) _____

Look at Paragraphs 21 to 24.

18. Why does the writer put the word "BUT" in capital letters at the beginning of Paragraph 21?

_____

_____ | 2 | 1 | 0

19. In the opinion of Francisco Gil-White, what important influence have celebrities replaced?

_____ | 2 | ■ | 0

20. What does the writer's use of the expression "blazing a trail" (Paragraph 24) tell you about Gareth Gates and Tiger Woods?

_____

_____ | 2 | ■ | 0

[Turn over for Questions 21, 22 and 23 on *Page six*

PAGE TOTAL

Marks

Look at Paragraphs 25 to 28.

21. **In your own words** what, according to Maltby, could be the positive outcomes of admiring David Beckham?

_____

_____   2 1 0

22. According to Mark Griffiths:

    (*a*) how can idols form a healthy part of people's lives?

    Answer in your own words.

_____

_____   2 ■ 0

    (*b*) why have pop stars and film stars replaced political and religious leaders?
    Tick (✓) the appropriate box.

    They are good looking.   ☐

    They are easily recognised.   ☐

    They are respected and highly regarded. ☐   2 ■ 0

Think about the passage as a whole.

23. "DAZZLED BY THE STARS"

    Explain why, in your opinion, this is an **appropriate** title.

_____

_____

_____   2 1 0

[END OF QUESTION PAPER]

PAGE
TOTAL

[BLANK PAGE]

C

0860/405

NATIONAL
QUALIFICATIONS
2005

WEDNESDAY, 4 MAY
2.30 PM – 3.20 PM

ENGLISH
STANDARD GRADE
Credit Level
Reading
Text

Read carefully the passage overleaf. It will help if you read it twice. When you have done so, answer the questions. Use the spaces provided in the Question/Answer booklet.

SCOTTISH
QUALIFICATIONS
AUTHORITY

1   Rameses I Station, usually called Cairo Railway Station, is a century old, like the railway system itself, which stretches from Alexandria on the shores of the Mediterranean, to Aswan on the Upper Nile, at the northern edge of Lake Nasser—the border of Sudan on the south side. The design of the station is of interest, and it has been said that it represents the epitome of nineteenth-century Egyptian architects' desire to combine classical and Islamic building styles, in response to Khedive Ismail's plan to create a "European Cairo"—Moorish meets modern.

2   Kings, queens, princes, heads of state, and generals have arrived and departed here. One of Naguib Mahfouz's earliest heroes, the ultra-nationalist anti-British rabble rouser, Saad Zaghlul, escaped an assassination attempt at Cairo Station on his return from one of his numerous exiles, in 1924. Given Egypt's history of dramatic arrivals and departures the railway station figures as a focal point and a scene of many riotous send-offs and welcomes.

3   The best story about Cairo Railway Station, told to me by a man who witnessed it unfold, does not concern a luminary but rather a person delayed in the third class ticket queue. When this fussed and furious man at last got to the window he expressed his exasperation to the clerk, saying, "Do you know who I am?"

4   The clerk looked him up and down and, without missing a beat, said, "In that shabby suit, with a watermelon under your arm, and a Third Class ticket to El Minya, who could you possibly be?"

5   To leave the enormous sprawling dust-blown city of gridlock and gritty buildings in the sleeper to Aswan was bliss. It was quarter to eight on a chilly night. I sat down in my inexpensive First Class compartment, listened to the departure whistles, and soon we were rolling through Cairo. Within minutes we were at Gizeh—the ruins overwhelmed by the traffic and the bright lights, the tenements and bazaar; and in less than half an hour we were in open country; little settlements of square mud-block houses, fluorescent lights reflected in the canal beside the track, the blackness of the countryside at night, a mosque with a lighted minaret, now and then a solitary car or truck, and on one remote road about twenty men in white robes going home after prayers. In Cairo they would have been unremarkable, just part of the mob; here they looked magical, their robes seeming much whiter on the nighttime road, their procession much spookier for its orderliness, like a troop of sorcerers.

6   I went into the corridor and opened the train window to see the robed men better, and there I was joined by Walter Frakes from St Louis, an enormous man with a long mild face, and a smooth bag-like chin, who found his compartment small, "but what's the use of fussing?" He was travelling with his wife, Marylou, and another couple, the Norrises, Lenny and Marge, also from St Louis. They too were heading to Aswan to meet a boat and take a river cruise.

7   "And if I don't get a decent bed on that ship I'm going to be a wreck," Walter Frakes said. He was a very gentle man in spite of his size, which I took to be close to 300 pounds; and he was kindly and generally uncomplaining. All he said in the morning was: "Didn't get a wink of sleep. Tried to. Woke up every time the train stopped. Must have stopped a hundred times. Durn."

8   I had woken now and then as the train had slowed at crossings, or at the larger stations. There were sometimes flaring lights, barking dogs, otherwise the silence and the darkness of the Nile Valley, and a great emptiness: the vast and starry sky of the Egyptian desert, and that road south that ran alongside the train, the only road south, *the road to Johannesburg*.

9   In the bright early morning I saw a sign saying, *Kom-Ombo - 8 km*, indicating the direction to its lovely temple with a dual dedication, to Horus, the hawk-headed god, and Sobek, the croc-skulled deity. Another sign said, *Abu Simbel Macaroni*, and depicted its glutinous product in a red bowl.

10   Date palms in clusters, orange trees, low boxy houses, donkey carts piled high with tomatoes, the occasional camel, the men in white gowns and skullcaps, the boys walking to the fields carrying farm implements, and the wide slow river and the flat bright land shimmering under the blue sky. This was new Egypt but it was also old Egypt, for I had seen many of these images in the Cairo Museum—the adzes and mattocks the boys carried I had seen looking much the same, and the same heavy browed bullocks I had seen hammered in gold or carved in stone I saw browsing by the river; the same dogs with upright tails and big ears, the same narrow cats, and had I seen a snake or a croc they would have had counterparts in gold on a chariot or else mummified and mouldering in a museum case.

11   Some of those cap and gowned men were seated in groups eating pieces of bread loaves the same shape I had seen in the museum removed intact, solid and stale, from ancient tombs; the same fava beans that had been disinterred from crypts were being gobbled up from wagons of men selling *foul*, the stewed beans that are still an Egyptian staple. The same-shaped ewers and pitchers and bowls I had seen as old artefacts were visible here in the hands of women faffing around at the kitchen doors of their huts.

12   The Nile was near, about 300 yards from bank to bank, slow moving and light brown, showing clouds on its surface, with green fields on either side, some with marked-out plots and others divided into date plantations, hawks drifting over them on the wind currents, and in the river feluccas with sails—impossible to see these sails and not think of gulls' wings. And then, as though indicating we were approaching a populous place, there was a succession of cemeteries, great long slopes of sun-baked graves, and the grave markers, small rectangles set into the stony ground, with raised edges, like a whole hillside of truckle beds where the dead people lay. Beyond the next hill was Aswan.

Adapted from *Dark Star Safari* by Paul Theroux

[*END OF PASSAGE*]

[BLANK PAGE]

FOR OFFICIAL USE

C

Total
Mark

0860/406

NATIONAL
QUALIFICATIONS
2005

WEDNESDAY, 4 MAY
2.30 PM – 3.20 PM

ENGLISH
STANDARD GRADE
Credit Level
Reading
Questions

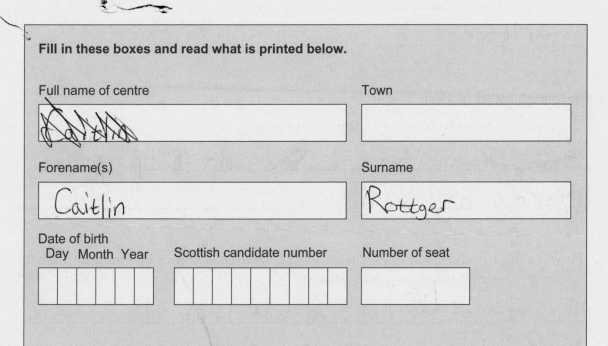

Fill in these boxes and read what is printed below.

Full name of centre

Town

Forename(s)

Caitlin

Surname

Rottger

Date of birth
Day Month Year

Scottish candidate number

Number of seat

**NB Before leaving the examination room you must give this booklet to the invigilator.
If you do not, you may lose all the marks for this paper.**

SCOTTISH
QUALIFICATIONS
AUTHORITY

©

QUESTIONS

Write your answers in the spaces provided.

Look at Paragraphs 1 and 2.

1. In your own words, what do Rameses I Station and the railway system have in common?

They are both ~~this~~ 100 years old ✓

2 ■ **0**

2. Why, in your opinion, does the writer use a long opening sentence?

To set the scene and describe geographically where the train goes to.

2 ■ **0**

3. Quote **one** word from Paragraph 1 which clearly indicates that the station is everything which nineteenth-century Egyptian architects believed in.

> epitome

2 ■ 0

4. "Moorish meets modern."

Comment on the effectiveness of this expression.

~~Its~~ effective because ~~this~~ sums ~~it~~ up ~~the~~ previous long sentence

2 1 0

5. How do the structure and word choice of the opening sentence of Paragraph 2 help to convey the importance of Cairo Station?

The use of long list ~~or~~ and word choice of importants persons shows importance of Cairo Station

2 1 0

6. Quote **two expressions** from Paragraph 2 which help to convey the idea of Cairo Station's dramatic history.

(i) "rabble rouser"

(ii) "assasination attempt"

2 1 0

10

PAGE
TOTAL

Marks

Look at Paragraphs 3 and 4.

7. In your own words, explain what is surprising about the best story the writer has heard about Cairo Railway Station.

   It involves an ordinary person not a dignatory

   ② 0

Look at Paragraph 5.

8. Quote **one** word from Paragraph 5 which sums up the writer's feelings on leaving Cairo.

bliss

   ② 0

9. In your own words, give **two** contrasts the writer notices on his journey from Cairo to the Egyptian countryside.

   ② 1 0

   (i) Cairo was congested whereas the country was not

   (ii) He saw fluorescent lights on his journey whereas in the country it was dark

10. "like a troop of sorcerers" (Paragraph 5).

    Explain the effectiveness of this simile.

    effective because it

    2 1 ⓪

Look at Paragraphs 6 to 9.

11. The writer describes Walter Frakes as kindly and generally uncomplaining.

    How does he illustrate this in Paragraphs 6 and 7?

    By quoting what Walter Frakes said which was optimistic and

    2 1 ⓪

    [Turn over

6

PAGE
TOTAL

Marks

12. In your own words, how had the writer spent the overnight journey?

He was awakened when the train was crawling over crossings and at the bigger stations

2 1 0

13. Explain the different use of the italics in:

(a) "*the road to Johannesburg*" (Paragraph 8).

_____

2 ■ 0

(b) "*Kom-Ombo - 8 km*" (Paragraph 9).

It's telling you the temple "Kom-Ombo" is 8km away

2 ■ 0

Look at Paragraphs 10 and 11.

14. What kind of impression does the writer create in the opening sentence of Paragraph 10?

It was a town with a lot of markets and the small businesses like fruit stalls

2 1 0

15. "This was new Egypt but it was also old Egypt," (Paragraph 10)

(a) In your own words, explain fully why it was possible for the writer to say this.

He had looked at a lot of these pictures in the museum in Cairo

2 1 0

(b) How does the writer continue this idea in Paragraph 11?

He says that the bread being eaten was what he saw in the museum.

2 1 0

16. Explain what is unusual about the word choice in the final sentence of Paragraph 11.

He refers to the "women faffing around"

_____

2 1 0

Marks

Look at Paragraph 12.

17. (a) Tick (✓) the appropriate box to show which of the following statements best reflects the writer's description of the Nile.

It is muddy and polluted. ☐

It is fertile and tranquil. ✓

It is narrow and unimpressive. ☐

②■ 0

(b) Justify your choice with close reference to the paragraph.

~~Trang~~ A "tranquil" river could mean "a slow-moving" river and "the green fields on either side" suggests it's "fertile" ground next to it.

②1 0

18. Why might the sails on the boats make the writer think of gulls' wings? Give **two** reasons.

②1 0

(i) They both ~~have similar~~ flap in ⊕ wind

(ii) They are both similar colour = white

19. (a) What effect does the writer create in the final sentence of the passage?

He ~~finish finish~~ is finishing the journey he was describing and ~~sums~~ sums up the journey by saying he's nearly there

②■ 0

(b) How does the writer create this effect?

_____

_____

_____

2 1 ⓪

[Turn over for Question 20 on *Page six*

8

PAGE
TOTAL

Marks

Think about the passage as a whole.

20. The writer of the passage is someone who has an interest in both **history** and **travel**. With close reference to the passage show how he has conveyed this to the reader.

History _Throughout the journey he describes many historical facts as he observes and compares modern and historical happenings._

2 1 (0)

Travel _He is ~~is~~ traveling through Egypt and he_

2 1 (0)

[END OF QUESTION PAPER]

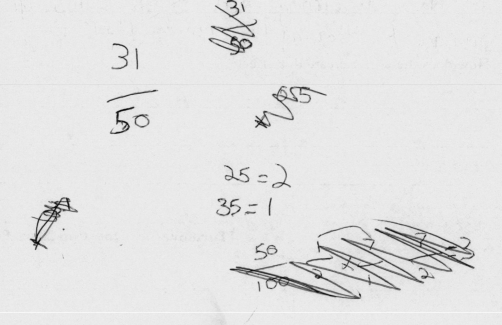

PAGE
TOTAL

[BLANK PAGE]

G

0860/403

NATIONAL
QUALIFICATIONS
2006

WEDNESDAY, 3 MAY
1.00 PM – 1.50 PM

ENGLISH
STANDARD GRADE
General Level
Reading
Text

Read carefully the passage overleaf. It will help if you read it twice. When you have done so,
answer the questions. Use the spaces provided in the Question/Answer booklet.

SCOTTISH
QUALIFICATIONS
AUTHORITY

©

SA 0860/403 6/67270

In this extract from a novel set in a secondary school, the narrator, John, is sitting in his Maths class. Gloria (nicknamed Glory Hallelujah) is another pupil in the same class.

1   I am sitting in school, in Maths, with a piece of paper in my hand. No, it is not my algebra homework. It is not a quiz that I have finished and am waiting to hand in to Mrs Moonface. The piece of paper in my hand has nothing at all to do with Mathematics. Nor does it have to do with any school subject. Nor is it really a piece of paper at all.

2   It is really my fate, masquerading as paper.

3   I am sitting next to Glory Hallelujah and I am waiting for a break in the action. Mrs Moonface is at the front of the room, going on about integers. I am not hearing a single thing that she is saying. She could stop lecturing about integers and start doing a cancan kick or singing a rap song and I would not notice.

4   She could call on me and ask me any question on earth, and I would not be able to answer.

5   But luckily, she does not call on me. She has a piece of chalk in her right hand. She is waving it around like a dagger as she spews algebra gibberish at a hundred miles a minute.

6   I hear nothing. Algebra does not have the power to penetrate my feverish isolation.

7   You see, I am preparing to ask Glory Hallelujah out on a date.

8   I am on an island, even though I am sitting at my desk surrounded by my classmates.

9   I am on Torture Island.

10   There are no trees on Torture Island—no huts, no hills, no beaches. There is only doubt.

11   Gloria will laugh at me. That thought is my lonely and tormenting company here on Torture Island. The exact timing and nature of her laughter are open to endless speculation.

12   She may not take me seriously. Her response may be "Oh, John, do you exist? Are you here on earth with me? I wasn't aware we were sharing the same universe."

13   Or she may be even more sarcastic. "John, I would love to go on a date with you, but I'm afraid I have to change my cat's litter box that night ."

14   So, as you can see, Torture Island is not exactly a beach resort. I am not having much fun here. I am ready to seize my moment and leave Torture Island forever.

15   In registration, I ripped a piece of paper from my yellow notepad. My black ball-point pen shook slightly in my trembling right hand as I wrote out the fateful question: "Gloria, will you go out with me this Friday?" Beneath that monumental question, I drew two boxes. One box was conspicuously large. I labelled it the YES box. The second box was tiny. I labelled it the NO box.

16   And that is the yellow piece of paper I have folded up into a square and am holding in my damp hand as I wait here on Torture Island for Mrs Moonface to turn towards the blackboard and give me the opportunity I need.

17   I cannot approach Glory Hallelujah after class because she is always surrounded by her friends. I cannot wait and pass the note to her later in the week because she may make plans to go out with one of her girlfriends. No, it is very evident to me that today is the day, and that I must pass the note before this period ends or forever live a coward.

18   There are only ten minutes left in Maths and Mrs Moonface seems to have no intention of recording her algebraic observations for posterity. Perhaps the piece of yellow chalk in her hand is just a prop. It is possible that the previous night she hurt her wrist in an arm-wrestling competition and can no longer write. It is also possible that she has forgotten all about her pupils and believes that she is playing a part in a Hollywood movie.

19   There are only seven minutes left in Maths. I attempt to turn Mrs Moonface towards the blackboard by telekinesis. The atoms of her body prove remarkably resistant to my telepathic powers.

20   There are six minutes left. Now there are five.

21   Mrs Moonface, for Pete's sake, write something on the blackboard! That is what Mathematics teachers do! Write down axioms, simplify equations, draw rectangles, measure angles, even, if you must, sketch the sneering razor-toothed face of Algebra itself. WRITE ANYTHING!

22   Suddenly Mrs Moonface stops lecturing.

23   Her right hand, holding the chalk, rises.

24   Then her hips begin to pivot.

25   This all unfolds in very slow motion. The sheer importance of the moment slows the action way, way down.

26   The pivoting of Mrs Moonface's hips causes a corresponding rotation in the plane of her shoulders and upper torso.

27   Her neck follows her shoulders, as day follows night.

28   Eventually, the lunar surface of her face is pulled towards the blackboard.

29   She begins to write. I have no idea what she is writing. It could be hieroglyphics and I would not notice. It could be a map to Blackbeard's treasure and I would not care.

30   I am now primed. My heart is thumping against my ribs, one by one, like a hammer pounding out a musical scale on a metal keyboard. Bing. Bang. Bong. Bam. I am breathing so quickly that I cannot breathe, if that makes any sense.

31   I am aware of every single one of my classmates in Maths.

32   Everyone in Maths is now preoccupied. There are only four minutes left in the period. Mrs Moonface is filling up blackboard space at an unprecedented speed, no doubt trying to scrape every last kernel of mathematical knowledge from the corncob of her brain before the bell. My classmates are racing to keep up with her. All around me pens are moving across notebooks at such a rate that ink can barely leak out and affix itself to paper.

33   My moment is at hand! The great clapper in the bell of fate clangs for me! *Ka-wang! Ka-wang!*

34   My right hand rises and begins to move sideways, very slowly, like a submarine, travelling at sub-desk depth to avoid teacher radar.

35   My right index finger makes contact with the sacred warm left wrist of Glory Hallelujah!

36   She looks down to see who is touching her at sub-desk depth. Spots my hand, with its precious yellow note.

37   Gloria understands instantly.

38   The exchange of the covert note is completed in a nanoinstant. Mrs Moonface and the rest of our Maths class have no idea that anything momentous has taken place.

39   I reverse the speed and direction of my right hand, and it returns safely to port.

40   Gloria has transferred my note to her lap and has moved her right elbow to block anyone on that side of her from seeing. The desk itself provides added shielding.

41   In the clever safe haven that she has created, she unfolds my note. Reads it.

42   She does not need to speak. She does not need to check the YES or NO boxes on my note. If she merely blinks, I will understand. If she wrinkles her nose, the import of her nose wrinkle will not be lost on me. In fact, so total is my concentration in that moment of grand suspense I am absolutely positive that there is nothing that Glory Hallelujah can do, no reaction that she can give off, that I will not immediately and fully understand.

43   I would stake my life on it.

44   But what she does do is this. She folds my note back up. Without looking at me—without even an eye blink or a nose wrinkle—she raises it to her lips. For one wild instant I think that she is going to kiss it.

45   Her pearly teeth part.

46   She eats my note.

Adapted from the novel "*You Dont Know Me*" By David Klass

[*END OF PASSAGE*]

G

Total
Mark

0860/404

NATIONAL
QUALIFICATIONS
2006

WEDNESDAY, 3 MAY
1.00 PM – 1.50 PM

ENGLISH
STANDARD GRADE
General Level
Reading
Questions

Fill in these boxes and read what is printed below.

Full name of centre

Town

Forename(s)

Surname

Date of birth
Day Month Year

Scottish candidate number

Number of seat

**NB Before leaving the examination room you must give this booklet to the invigilator.
If you do not, you may lose all the marks for this paper.**

SCOTTISH
QUALIFICATIONS
AUTHORITY

QUESTIONS

Write your answers in the spaces provided.

Look at Paragraphs 1 to 4.

1. (*a*) Who is Mrs Moonface?

_____ **2 ■ 0**

   (*b*) Why do you think John gives her the nickname "Mrs Moonface"?

_____
_____ **2 1 0**

2. "It is really my fate, masquerading as paper."

Why does the writer place this sentence in a paragraph of its own?

_____
_____ **2 1 0**

3. "Mrs Moonface is at the front of the room, going on about integers."

What does the expression "going on" suggest about John's attitude to what Mrs Moonface is saying?

_____ **2 ■ 0**

Look at Paragraphs 5 to 10.

4. How does the writer make Mrs Moonface's behaviour seem threatening?

_____
_____ **2 1 0**

PAGE TOTAL

Marks

5. ". . . spews algebra gibberish at a hundred miles a minute. . ." (Paragraph 5)

    Explain in your own words what the writer's word choice in this expression suggests about what John thinks of:

    (i) **what** she is saying

    _____

    _____   2 ■ 0

    (ii) **how** she says it

    _____

    _____   2 ■ 0

6. ". . . I am preparing to ask Glory Hallelujah out on a date." (Paragraph 7)

    Why do you think the writer waits until this point to reveal what John is planning to do?

    _____

    _____   2 1 0

7. "I am on Torture Island." (Paragraph 9)

    (*a*) **Explain fully in your own words** what the narrator means by this.

    _____

    _____   2 1 0

    (*b*) Write down an expression from later in the passage which contains a similar idea.

    ┌─────────────────────────────────────┐
    │   │
    └─────────────────────────────────────┘   2 ■ 0

    [Turn over

PAGE
TOTAL

Marks

8. Explain how the writer emphasises the bleakness of "Torture Island".

_____

_____

2 | 1 | 0

Look at Paragraphs 11 to 14.

9. (*a*) **Write down an example** of the writer's use of humour in these paragraphs.

_____

_____

2 | ■ | 0

(*b*) Explain why your chosen example is funny.

_____

_____

2 | 1 | 0

Look at Paragraphs 15 to 17.

10. Write down three pieces of evidence that suggest the narrator's nervousness at this point in the story.

_____

_____

_____

2 | 1 | 0

11. Quote **two** separate words used by the writer to suggest the importance of what John is asking Gloria.

```
┌────────────────┐   ┌────────────────┐
│                │   │                │
└────────────────┘   └────────────────┘
```

2 | 1 | 0

12. "One box was conspicuously large . . . The second box was tiny." (Paragraph 15)

Why do you think John makes the boxes different sizes?

_____

_____

2 | 1 | 0

PAGE TOTAL

Marks

13. **In your own words**, give a reason why John must make his approach to Gloria during Maths.

_____

_____

2 1 0

Look at Paragraphs 18 to 21.

14. How does the writer suggest the mood of increasing tension at this point in the passage?

_____

_____

2 ■ 0

15. "WRITE ANYTHING!" (Paragraph 21)

Why are these words written in capital letters?

_____

_____

2 ■ 0

Look at Paragraphs 22 to 33

16. (*a*) Identify any **one** technique used by the writer in this section to suggest John's growing excitement.

_____

2 ■ 0

(*b*) Explain **how** it does so.

_____

_____

2 1 0

[Turn over for Questions 17 to 20 on *Page six*

PAGE
TOTAL

Marks

Look at Paragraphs 34 to 46.

17. Give **three** reasons why Mrs Moonface is unaware of the note being passed.

_____

_____

_____   2 1 0

18. Why does John feel the "YES" or "NO" boxes on his note are now irrelevant?

_____

_____   2 1 0

19. How does the final paragraph provide an effective end to the passage?

_____

_____   2 1 0

Now look at the passage as a whole.

20. How realistic do you find the writer's description of this classroom incident? Give reasons for your opinion.

_____

_____

_____   2 1 0

[END OF QUESTION PAPER]

PAGE
TOTAL

[BLANK PAGE]

C

0860/405

NATIONAL
QUALIFICATIONS
2006

WEDNESDAY, 3 MAY
2.30 PM – 3.20 PM

ENGLISH
STANDARD GRADE
Credit Level
Reading
Text

Read carefully the passage overleaf. It will help if you read it twice. When you have done so, answer the questions. Use the spaces provided in the Question/Answer booklet.

SCOTTISH
QUALIFICATIONS
AUTHORITY

Casting a spell all over America

It's broadcast live on television and nine million children take part. **Alex Massie** gets out his dictionary and enters the world of the spelling bee.

1   Askay Buddiga had prepared thoroughly for this moment. The 13-year-old from Colorado Springs knew what was required of him. After all, his brother had won the Scripps Howard National Spelling Bee just two years earlier, and now he was here at the final. Perhaps the pressure of family expectation got to him for a moment. Perhaps he panicked.

2   Whatever the reason, when pronouncer Dr Jacques Bailly announced that the teenager's word in the sixth round of the competition was "alopecoid", Buddiga suddenly collapsed. The 1,000-strong audience gathered at the Hyatt hotel in downtown Washington DC was stunned. He had fainted.

3   But within 30 seconds he was back on his feet—calmly spelling a-l-o-p-e-c-o-i-d to much applause. Buddiga recovered sufficiently to go on to the final rounds of the competition.

4   Though it might seem arcane in the age of computer spellcheck programs, more than nine million American children took part in spelling contests this year, with the top 265 progressing to Washington for the grand finals last week.

5   With yellow numbered ID placards hung around their necks, the contestants looked as if they had been summoned to take part in a police line-up. One by one the youngsters stepped up to the microphone to hear and spell their words. Although they operated on a two-minute time limit, they could ask for alternative pronunciations, the definition and derivation of the word and ask for it to be used in a sentence. A contestant might be asked to spell such words as "widdershins", "hauberk", "putrescible", "gallimaufry" and "salicylate".

6   But the competition really got going when the field was whittled down to the final two dozen spellers on day three. By then, contestants were beginning to struggle as they tiptoed, letter by letter, through their words as though they were crossing a minefield. "Vimineous" ended North Carolina's Simon Winchester challenge.

"Parrhesia" did the same for Nichols James Truelson, who slumped back into his chair with a bemused, vacant look on his face as the audience applauded sympathetically. But the greatest ovation was reserved for Buddiga, who eventually stumbled on "schwarmerei", but still managed to finish runner-up.

7   The bee is televised live and makes for oddly gripping television. The merciless nature of the competition, where a single misplaced consonant or forgotten vowel ejects a speller from the contest, gives proceedings a kind of high-wire drama as the spellers fret their way through the rounds, each more difficult than the last. It might seem an unlikely ratings success, but it certainly beats the world wood-chopping championships.

8   Some parents are tempted to take their child's preparation for the bee to extraordinary, obsessive lengths. It's a perennial cliché of American sportswriting but there's more than a hint of truth in the old phrase that in the land of the free, only winners are remembered.

9   And spelling is on the up. The remarkable success of the documentary *Spellbound*, which followed eight spellers to the bee and was nominated for an Academy Award last year, brought the competition to a new audience.

10   *Spellbound* featured one boy, Neil, whose father hired specialist tutors to coach his son in words derived from French and German. Despite such dedication, Neil didn't win.

11   But the proclivities of such contestants and their parents in no way represent the general participant. "It's not just the geeks and the nerds. These are normal kids," says Ohio's Beth Richards, whose daughter, Bailey, was making her second appearance in the finals. "This is the Superbowl of words."

12   While runner-up Buddiga sat quietly, hands in pockets and with the stern spelling equivalent of a poker face, his rival, 14-year-old David Tidmarsh from South Bend, Indiana, was running on nervous energy, fidgeting constantly and squinting into the

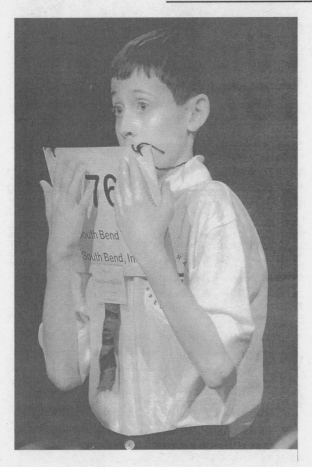

David Tidmarsh of Indiana just minutes away from winning the National Spelling Bee

distance as he worked out the correct spelling of the championship word. He would be champion if he could successfully spell "autochthonous" (meaning indigenous). "Could you use it in a sentence please?" he asked, as his voice rose an octave and he struggled to control his breathing.

13   He appeared close to hyperventilating as he started slowly then rattled through the word, confident that, after three days of ruthless competition, the grand prize was his. Blinking in amazement, he appeared overwhelmed, burying his face in his hands as his mother rushed the stage to embrace him. "It's kind of sad I won't be able to be in more spelling bees," says Tidmarsh. The tears welled in his eyes as he contemplated the awful void that lay ahead. Unlike boxers or basketball stars there's no second coming or return from retirement available to champion spellers. Former winners are not eligible to enter.

14   On the other hand, spellers leave on a high note and neither they nor their audience are likely to be humbled and saddened by the sight of an ageing champion dragging his weary body into the ring for one final ignominious battle against fresher faced opponents.

15   Tidmarsh's father Jay, a law professor, appeared almost as nervous as his son as he paced around the outer edge of the Hyatt hotel ballroom, unable to keep still or watch proceedings with equanimity. "I never actually thought about what it would be like to win. I guess I just couldn't believe it. It was just really surreal," says his son, after being presented with the trophy and cheques worth $17,000. "My parents will probably put it in a savings account," he adds, his voice tinged with resignation. "But I'll try and get hold of some of it to spend at the mall."

16   Tidmarsh was the first winner from Indiana since 1928 and his triumph was front page news and the subject of numerous editorials in his home state's newspapers. "It's this great slice of Americana," says the 1979 champion Katie Kerwin McCrimmon, who now commentates on the bee for television. "You come home, and there are banners at the airport and signs in the streets."

17   Robert Rappoport, from Albany, New York, whose son Paul was eliminated in the second round, says: "There are no second chances and only one winner. This is the real thing. There are only probably a few who are really in with a chance of winning and who become obsessed with the bee. Most of the competitors are just bright kids who like to read."

18   A cursory survey of the contestants' names—Chen, Srinivasan, Biedermann, Ofori, Milovac, Irwinsky, Menendez, McMahon— points to one reason for the bee's popularity. It is the personification of the American melting pot and gives substance to the American dream. If you want it enough and work hard enough you can succeed in America.

19   Outside the Hyatt Hotel a ragbag collection of protestors from the Simplified Spelling Society waving placards proclaiming "I'm thru with through" and "50,000,000 illiterates can't be wrong" pressed leaflets arguing for an overhaul of spelling upon dubious and somewhat nonplussed contestants.

20   For David Tidmarsh and his fellow contestants, however, there's nothing wrong with the language as it stands. During an impromptu press conference he was asked if all this was as good as Hollywood can make it.

21   The young champion thought for a second before a goofy grin spread across his face: "It's even better."

Adapted from an article in
The Scotsman

[*END OF PASSAGE*]

[BLANK PAGE]

C

FOR OFFICIAL USE

Total Mark

0860/406

NATIONAL
QUALIFICATIONS
2006

WEDNESDAY, 3 MAY
2.30 PM – 3.20 PM

ENGLISH
STANDARD GRADE
Credit Level
Reading
Questions

Fill in these boxes and read what is printed below.

Full name of centre

Town

Forename(s)

Caitlin

Surname

Rottger

Date of birth
Day Month Year

Scottish candidate number

Number of seat

**NB Before leaving the examination room you must give this booklet to the invigilator.
If you do not, you may lose all the marks for this paper.**

SCOTTISH
QUALIFICATIONS
AUTHORITY

QUESTIONS

Write your answers in the spaces provided.

Marks

Look at Paragraphs 1 to 3.

1. (*a*) In what sort of a contest is Askay Buddiga taking part?

   A Spelling bee ✓

   ② ■ 0

   (*b*) Give **three** reasons why Askay might have expected to do well.

   • Brother won 2 years ago
   • He was in the final
   • He ~~has~~ had practiced for it

   ② 1 0

2. "He had fainted." (Paragraph 2)

   How does the writer signal the dramatic nature of this event to the reader?

   He puts it into a short sentence ~~on its own~~

   ② 1 0

3. **In your own words**, what might have been the reasons for Askay's fainting?

   He might have gotten scared or was worried
   about what his family expected of him

   ② 1 0

4. "a-l-o-p-e-c-o-i-d" (Paragraph 3)

   Why does the writer separate the letters in this word with dashes?

   To show he's spelling the word

   how

   ② ■ 0

PAGE
TOTAL

Marks

Look at Paragraphs 4 to 6.

5. "Though it might seem arcane . . ." (Paragraph 4)

    Explain in your own words why spelling contests might seem "arcane" or strange.

    <u>Because in the 20th century there is</u>
    <u>technology that can spell for us.</u>

    (2) (1) 0

6. ". . . contestants looked as though they had been summoned to take part in a police line-up." (Paragraph 5)

    What does this description suggest about how the contestants may have been feeling?

    <u>That they were feeling nervous</u>

    (2) ■ 0

7. **In your own words**, explain what **four** things each contestant could ask for to help them with the spelling of a word.

    <u>They could ask for the meaning where the</u>
    <u>word comes from, different ways of saying</u>
    <u>the word and the word to be put into</u>
    <u>context.</u>

    (2) 1 0

    [Turn over

6

PAGE
TOTAL

Marks

8. "as though they were crossing a minefield" (Paragraph 6)

 (a) Identify the figure of speech the writer is using here.

 Simile

 (2) 0

 (b) **In your own words**, explain how appropriate you find the use of this image.

 It sums up the sentence ~~before~~ and there is as link between the simile and the use of the word tiptoed.

 2 1 (0)

 (c) Write down an expression used later in the passage which contains a similar idea to ". . . crossing a minefield".

 "Who eventually stumbled on"

 2 (0)

Look at Paragraphs 8 to 11.

9. "Some parents are tempted to take their child's preparation for the bee to extraordinary, obsessive lengths." (Paragraph 8)

 Give a reason why some parents are prepared to behave in this way.

 Because there childs success might be a reflection on them so people think they're successful

 2 (0)

10. How does the first sentence of Paragraph 11 act as a link between Paragraphs 10 and 11?

 Because in paragraph 10 the writer describes what lengths parents may go to help their child win "hired specialist tutors" whereas paragraph 11 is the opposit in saying that not everybody goes to those lengths.

 2 1 (0)

2

PAGE TOTAL

Marks

Look at Paragraphs 12 to 15.

11. **In your own words**, explain fully the differing reactions of David Tidmarsh and Askay Buddiga in Paragraph 12.

   (i) **Buddiga:**

    He had a blank face, ~~his~~ ~~face~~ looked like he was concentrating.

          2 ① 0

   (ii) **Tidmarsh:**

    He was moving a lot, - looked scared

          2 ① 0

12. "... the awful void that lay ahead." (Paragraph 13)

   (a) What is the "awful void" that lies ahead of Tidmarsh?

    That he won't be able to compete in spelling bee any more

          ② ■ 0

   (b) What tone is the writer adopting in the expression?

    ~~Is~~ A sad tone

          2 ■ ⓪

13. "Former winners are not eligible to enter." (Paragraph 13)

   In your own words, explain how the writer illustrates the advantages of this rule in paragraph 14.

   They are ~~xx~~ number one when they have to stop competing

          ② 1 0

Look at Paragraphs 16 to 21.

14. "It's this great slice of Americana" (Paragraph 16)

   What do you think Katie Kerwin McCrimmon means by this?

   It's a success when you win the competition it's a good feeling.

          2 1 ⓪

[Turn over

6

PAGE TOTAL

Marks

15. "It is the personification of the American melting pot . . ." (Paragraph 18)

How does the writer illustrate this idea in Paragraph 18?

By using the metaphor "it is"

2 1 ⓪

16. What does the writer's use of the words "ragbag collection" to describe the protestors suggest about his attitude towards them?

That he doesn't like them or Value them

② ■ 0

17. "I'm thru with through" (Paragraph 19)

Explain the **two** different spellings of the word "through" on the protestors' placards.

They are using "thru" because they are making a point and saying that they don't want or need to spell "through" correctly.

2 ① 0

18. **In your own words**, explain the contestants' reaction to the protestors.

They don't care and they think that the words are fine as they are.

2 ■ ⓪

Think about the passage as a whole.

19. Quote **three** expressions from the passage which convey the view that the contestants are really no different from other children.

"These are normal kids"
"to spend at the mall"
"bright kids who like to read"

② 1 0

5

PAGE
TOTAL

Marks

20. Why is "Casting a spell all over America" a good title for this article?

Because it's a play on words and it ~~a~~ tells you it's about America ~~and~~

2 1 (0)

[*END OF QUESTION PAPER*]

$$\frac{28}{50}$$

FOR OFFICIAL USE

p2	
p3	
p4	
p5	
p6	
p7	
TOTAL MARK	

[BLANK PAGE]

G

0860/403

NATIONAL
QUALIFICATIONS
2007

TUESDAY, 1 MAY
1.00 PM – 1.50 PM

ENGLISH
STANDARD GRADE
General Level
Reading
Text

Read carefully the passage overleaf. It will help if you read it twice. When you have done so, answer the questions. Use the spaces provided in the Question/Answer booklet.

SCOTTISH
QUALIFICATIONS
AUTHORITY

©

Biker Boys and Girls

There is only one "wall of death" doing the rounds at British fairs today. But a new generation of daredevil riders is intent on keeping the show on (or rather, off) the road.

1   Last year Kerri Cameron, aged 19 and a little bored with her job as a horse-riding instructor, was looking up job vacancies on the internet. Puzzled, she turned to her mother and said, "Mum, what's a wall of death?"

2   Her mother, Denise, a health worker who has always had a horror of motorcycles, told her that walls of death were places where people rode motorbikes round the insides of a 20 ft-high wooden drum and tried not to fall off and get killed. "Gosh," said Kerri, "that sounds fun."

3   She picked up her mobile, phoned the number mentioned on the internet and then arranged to see Ken Fox, owner of the wall of death. Ken Fox didn't ask about her school qualifications, only if she wanted a ride on the back of his bike around the wall. Yes, she said.

4   Ken Fox revved up the demonstration bike and spun it on to the 45-degree wooden apron that bridges the ground and the perpendicular wall and then took it three or four times around the lower bits of the wall itself just to see if she could cope. Then he went round with Kerri sitting on the handlebars. She passed that test, too. She thought it was fantastic. Unbelievable. The best!

5   A year later Kerri is doing 20 shows a day, driving a skeletal aluminium go-kart around Ken Fox's wall of death to within six inches of the safety wire at the top—the wire that's there to prevent the machines sailing off into the crowd. "It's much more fun than helping kids on horses," she says, giggling nervously and brushing a strand of blonde hair back behind her ear. "The only thing I really miss about home is flush toilets."

6   Ken Fox and his wife Julie, their sons, Luke and Alex, and their troupe of Kerri, a new girl rider called Emma Starr, a man who prefers to be known just as Philip, and a wall-of-death enthusiast of an accountant named Neil Calladine, now operate the last wall of death in business in Britain. Calladine is the wall's "spieler", stalking the front of the attraction with a microphone, promising thrills and excitement as Ken and Luke Fox sit on their bikes, creating the roaring throttle noises of impending danger. Later, Luke and his father dip and zig-zag their bikes across each other, spinning round the drum every four seconds, as the holiday crowds peer tentatively down over the safety wire and then, in the traditional way, shower coins into the ring after being told that wall-of-death riders can never get insurance. Each show lasts 20 minutes; at one stage four riders are zipping up, down and all around.

7   In the 1930s and 1940s there were almost 30 walls of death at seaside resorts and fairgrounds around the country, often competing side-by-side in fairgrounds; now there are four left. One is in a steam museum in Derbyshire, another is the hobby/toy of a Cornish builder, and a third is owned by a 54-year-old agricultural engineer who "has done everything in motorcycles except ridden a wall of death". That wall's old owner, Graham Cripsey, of the Cripsey fairground family, is coming down from Skegness to teach him how to ride it.

8   Only Ken Fox and his band, together with pet dog Freebie, two ferrets and two cockatiels, tour in the traditional way, squelching out of their winter quarters from behind the Cambridgeshire hedgerows just before Easter and heading in convoy for the first of the 6,000 miles they will complete by the end of October. Ken is lucky that Julie can drive one of the trucks, change the 2 ft-high tyres, make sure Alex does his school lessons on his laptop, cook, make sandwiches and dish out the £2 tickets. She, too, loves the travelling life. "When you think I used to be a dental nurse," she says, her eyes misting a little.

9   She also helped her husband build his wall of death. "My old wall was wearing out," he says, "so I bought a 200 ft section of very long,

very straight, Oregon pine that cost £70,000 (Oregon pine, one of the tallest trees in the world, is used for all walls of death because of the straightness of its grain and the lack of knot in its timber). I got the planks cut in a milling yard. I went to a boatyard where they built submarines. The place was so big we could have built 50 walls of death."

10   The motorbikes used for shows are Indian Scouts made in the 1920s by the Hendee Motorcycle Company of Springfield, Massachusetts, deliberately engineered for easy balance with all the controls on the left, so Chicago cops could use their right hands for drawing their revolvers and shooting at Al Capone-style gangsters. This means the bikes are perfect for tricks. Take your hand off the throttle of a modern motorbike and it slips back to idling mode, thus losing the power that keeps the bike on the wall. Take your hand off the throttle of an Indian Scout, and the revs stay as they are—which means that you can zoom round and round the wall of death, arms in the air, to your heart's content.

11   The first wall of death is said by Graham Cripsey to have come to Britain from America in 1928 with others close on its heels. His grandfather, Walter, and father, Roy, trained lions to ride in the sidecars, as did the famous George "Tornado" Smith at Southend's Kursaal fairground. The Cripseys also developed a technique of being towed round behind the Indian Scouts on roller skates. "If you were competing side by side in a fairground, you always had to have one stunt better than the other," explains Graham. Smith also kept a skeleton in a sidecar which, with a flick on a control, would suddenly sit bolt upright. And Ricky Abrey, 61, who rode with him as "The Black Baron", says Tornado perfected a ride where three riders would cut off their engines at the top of the wall and instantly re-start them again, causing the audience to gasp as 2 ft-long flashes of flame escaped the exhaust pipes.

12   Fun, then, for all the family. "People still love the wall of death," says Ken Fox emphatically. "People like what we put on and get good value for it. If they see it once, they always want to see it again. The problem is finding the people to work on it. There are a lot of soft men around."

13   "Wall of death" is, thankfully, a bit of a misnomer, for there have been no fatal accidents on British walls, though whether that's due to good luck or fear-induced careful preparation is difficult to tell. "I've been knocked off by other riders, the engine's stalled, I've had punctures and I've hit a safety cable," says Ken Fox, pointing at his scars. "Everyone gets falls at some time but we try to be spot-on in our preparations. Before every show we spend a complete day trying to get the machines working perfectly."

14   Luke Fox suffered his first bad fall last year, flicking a safety-cable bolt on one of his "dips" as he zig-zagged his bike up and down. He fell 20 ft, got up and started again, even though he'd severely torn his knee. In a sense, he's got his own good-luck charm. His Indian bike was originally ridden by no less a daredevil than Tornado Smith himself. Luke has also inherited his father's total dedication to the trade and the Fox family wall looks set to last into the immediate future. Indeed, he and Kerri are now a partnership, sharing the long-haul driving and other things, while young Alex, the ferret-fancier, is raring for his first go at the wall.

15   Even Neil Calladine, the spieler, has shed his accountant duties and can indulge his lifelong passion for fairgrounds, though he needs to talk almost non-stop from 2 pm to 10 pm each show day and consumes mountains of throat sweets. "I make sure I go back and see the missus once a month," he says, "and of course I'm there all winter. I suppose I'm one of those fortunate people whose hobby has become his life. I love the freedom of travel, no nine-to-five, just us and the open road."

16   In that he's just like Kerri Cameron, bless her daredevil heart.

Adapted from an article
by John Dodd

[END OF PASSAGE]

[BLANK PAGE]

FOR OFFICIAL USE

G

Total
Mark

0860/404

NATIONAL
QUALIFICATIONS
2007

TUESDAY, 1 MAY
1.00 PM – 1.50 PM

ENGLISH
STANDARD GRADE
General Level
Reading
Questions

Fill in these boxes and read what is printed below.

Full name of centre

Town

Forename(s)

Surname

Date of birth
Day Month Year   Scottish candidate number   Number of seat

**NB Before leaving the examination room you must give this booklet to the invigilator.
If you do not, you may lose all the marks for this paper.**

SCOTTISH
QUALIFICATIONS
AUTHORITY

SA 0860/404 6/75170

©

Marks

QUESTIONS

Write your answers in the spaces provided.

Look at Paragraphs 1 to 3.

1. **In your own words**, explain fully why Kerri Cameron was looking up job vacancies on the internet.

    _____

    `2 | 1 | 0`

2. What is surprising about Kerri's reaction to what her mother tells her about the wall of death?

    _____

    _____

    `2 | 1 | 0`

3. Why do you think Ken Fox was not interested in Kerri's school qualifications?

    _____

    _____

    `2 | ■ | 0`

Look at Paragraphs 4 and 5.

4. How does the writer suggest Kerri's enthusiasm after her test on the bike:

    (*a*)   by word choice?

    _____

    `2 | ■ | 0`

    (*b*)   by sentence structure?

    _____

    `2 | ■ | 0`

5. **Using your own words as far as possible**, describe **two** aspects of Kerri's performance which could be described as dangerous.

    _____

    _____

    `2 | 1 | 0`

PAGE
TOTAL

Marks

Look at Paragraph 6.

6. **In your own words**, explain the job of the "spieler".

_____

2 1 0

7. ". . . shower coins into the ring . . ."

   Give **two** reasons why "shower" is an effective word to use in this context.

_____

_____

2 1 0

8. Why do you think members of the audience are told that wall-of-death riders "can never get insurance"?

_____

2 ■ 0

9. Explain fully what the expression "zipping up, down and all around" suggests about the riders' performance.

_____

_____

2 1 0

Look at Paragraphs 7 to 9.

10. How does the writer illustrate the decline in popularity of walls of death?

_____

2 1 0

[Turn over

PAGE
TOTAL

Marks

11. "Only Ken Fox and his band . . ." (Paragraph 8)

    Write down **one** word from earlier in the passage which contains the same idea as "band".

    2 ■ 0

12. Explain fully why you think the writer uses the word "squelching" in Paragraph 8.

    _____

    _____

    2 1 0

13. Look again at the sentence which begins "Ken is lucky . . ." (Paragraph 8).

    How does the structure of the **whole** sentence help to reinforce how busy Julie is between Easter and October?

    _____

    _____

    2 1 0

14. Why is Oregon pine so suitable for walls of death?

    _____

    2 1 0

Look at Paragraph 10.

15. **Using your own words as far as possible**, explain why the Indian Scout bikes are "perfect for tricks."

    _____

    _____

    2 1 0

PAGE
TOTAL

Marks

16. Identify two techniques used by the writer which help to involve the reader in his description of the Indian Scout motorbikes. **Quote evidence** from the paragraph to support your answers.

Technique	Evidence

2 1 0

2 1 0

Look at Paragraphs 11 and 12.

17. Why might the nicknames "Tornado" and "The Black Baron" be suitable for wall-of-death riders?

Tornado

_____

The Black Baron

_____

2 1 0

[Turn over

PAGE
TOTAL

Marks

18. (*a*) Write down **four** things the early wall-of-death riders included in their acts.

_____

_____

_____

_____

2 1 0

(*b*) **In your own words**, give **two** reasons why such things were included in the acts.

_____

_____

2 1 0

Look at Paragraphs 13 to 16.

19. ". . . is, thankfully, a bit of a misnomer, . . ." (Paragraph 13)

(*a*) Tick (✓) the box beside the best definition of "misnomer".

old-fashioned attraction	
risky venture	
successful show	
wrongly applied name	

(*b*) Write down evidence from the passage to support your answer to 19(*a*).

_____

2 1 0

20. Why is the word "dips" (Paragraph 14) in inverted commas?

_____

2 ■ 0

PAGE
TOTAL

Marks

21. Give **three** pieces of evidence to support the writer's statement that "the Fox family wall looks set to last into the immediate future" (Paragraph 14).

_____

_____

_____   2 1 0

22. Show how the final paragraph is an effective conclusion to this article.

_____

_____   2 1 0

[END OF QUESTION PAPER]

PAGE TOTAL

FOR OFFICIAL USE

p2 ☐

p3 ☐

p4 ☐

p5 ☐

p6 ☐

p7 ☐

TOTAL
MARK ☐

[BLANK PAGE]

C

0860/405

NATIONAL
QUALIFICATIONS
2007

TUESDAY, 1 MAY
2.30 PM – 3.20 PM

ENGLISH
STANDARD GRADE
Credit Level
Reading
Text

Read carefully the passage overleaf. It will help if you read it twice. When you have done so, answer the questions. Use the spaces provided in the Question/Answer booklet.

SCOTTISH
QUALIFICATIONS
AUTHORITY

DARKNESS AND LIGHT

In this passage Kathleen Jamie describes a visit to Maes Howe, one of the most important archaeological sites on Orkney. Her visit takes place in December, just before the winter solstice—the shortest day of the year.

1   The building nowadays known as Maes Howe is a Neolithic chambered cairn, a tomb where, 5000 years ago, they interred the bones of the dead. In its long, long existence it has been more forgotten about than known, but in our era it is open to the public, with tickets and guides and explanatory booklets. It stands, a mere grassy hump in a field, in the central plain of Mainland Orkney. There is a startling collection of other Neolithic sites nearby.

2   To reach Maes Howe I took the road that passes over a thin isthmus between two lochs. On the west side is a huge brooding stone circle, the Ring of Brodgar. On the east, like three elegant women conversing at a cocktail party, are the Standing Stones of Stenness. The purpose of these may be mysterious, but a short seven miles away is the Neolithic village called Skara Brae. There is preserved a huddle of roofless huts, dug half underground into midden and sand dune. There, you can marvel at the domestic normality, that late Stone Age people had beds and cupboards and neighbours and beads. You can feel both their presence, their day-to-day lives, and their utter absence. It's a good place to go. It re-calibrates your sense of time.

3   Two men were standing at the car park at Maes Howe. The taller, older man was wearing a white shirt and improbable tartan trousers. As I stepped out of the car, he shook his head sadly. The younger man was dressed for outdoors, somewhat like a traffic warden, with a woollen hat pulled down to his eyes and a navy-blue coat. For a moment we all looked at each other. The taller man spoke first.

4   "Not looking good, I'm afraid."

5   The timing was right, the sun was setting, but . . .

6   "Cloud," said the tall man.

7   "Can't be helped," I replied.

8   "Will you go in, anyway? You can't always tell, you just need a moment when the cloud breaks . . ."

9   Alan, an Englishman in Historic Scotland tartan trousers, led me into a little shop to issue a ticket. The shop was housed in an old water mill, some distance from the tomb, and sold guidebooks and fridge magnets and tea towels. From the window you could see over the main road to the tomb.

10   "Tell you what," he said. "I'll give you a ticket so you can come back tomorrow, if you like, but I can't give you one for the actual solstice, Saturday. We start selling them at two-thirty on the actual solstice. It's first come, first served."

11   "How many people come?"

12   "Well, we can accommodate 25, at a pinch."

13   But today there was only myself.

14   The young guide, Rob, was waiting outside. A workman's van hurtled past, then we crossed the road, entered through a wicket gate and followed a path across the field. We were walking toward the tomb by an indirect route that respected the wide ditch around the site. Sheep were grazing the field, and a heron was standing with its aristocratic back to us. There was a breeze, and the shivery call of a curlew descending. On all sides there are low hills, holding the plain between them. To the

south, the skyline is dominated by two much bigger, more distant hills, a peak and a plateau. Though you wouldn't know it from here, they belong to another island, to Hoy. Above these dark hills, in horizontal bars, were the offending clouds.

＊ ＊ ＊

15 You enter into the inner chamber of the tomb by a low passageway more than 25 feet long. It's more of a journey than a gateway. You don't have to crawl on hands and knees, but neither can you walk upright. The stone roof bears down on your spine; a single enormous slab of stone forms the wall you brush with your left shoulder. You must walk in that stooped position just a moment too long, so when you're admitted to the cairn two sensations come at once: you're glad to stand, and the other is a sudden appreciation of stone. You are admitted into a solemn place.

16 You are standing in a high, dim stone vault. There is a thick soundlessness, like a recording studio, or a strongroom. A moment ago, you were in the middle of a field, with the wind and curlews calling. That world has been taken away, and the world you have entered into is not like a cave, but a place of artifice, of skill. Yes, that's it, what you notice when you stand and look around is cool, dry, applied skill. Across five thousand years you can still feel their self-assurance.

17 The walls are of red sandstone, dressed into long rectangles, with a tall sentry-like buttress in each corner to support the corbelled roof. The passage to the outside world is at the base of one wall. Set waist-high into the other three are square openings into cells which disappear into the thickness of the walls. That's where they laid the dead, once the bones had been cleaned of flesh by weather and birds. The stone blocks which would once have sealed these graves lie on the gravel floor. And the point is, the ancients who built this tomb lined it up precisely: the long passageway faces exactly the setting midwinter sun. Consequently, for the few days around the winter solstice a beam of the setting sun shines along the passage, and onto the tomb's back wall. In recent years, people have crept along the passageway at midwinter to witness this. Some, apparently, find it overwhelming.

＊ ＊ ＊

18 We crossed the field. The heron took to the air. I dawdled behind. My guide, the young Rob, was waiting at the entrance, which is just a low square opening at the bottom of the mound. I glanced back at the outside world, the road, the clouded sky over Hoy's hills, which did not look promising; then we crept inside and for a long minute walked doubled over, until Rob stood and I followed.

19 Inside was bright as a tube train, and the effect was brutal. I'd expected not utter darkness, but perhaps a dullish red. Rob was carrying a torch but this light revealed every crack, every joint and fissure in the ancient stonework. At once a man's voice said, "Sorry, I'll switch it off," but the moment was lost and, anyway, I'd been forewarned. As he sold me the ticket, Alan had told me that surveyors were inside the cairn, with all their equipment. "A bit of a problem", was how he'd put it. And here they were. We entered the tomb and, in that fierce white light, it was like that moment which can occur in midlife, when you look at your mother and realise with a shock that she is old.

20 The surveyors were doing a project that involved laser-scanning, photogrammetry, and pulse-radar inspection. They were working inside the tomb, and had been for days. A huge implement, I couldn't tell if it was a torch or a camera, lay on a schoolroom chair. There was a telephone in one of the grave-cells. There were two surveyors. One was folded, foetus-like, into the little cell in the back wall. I could see only his legs. He grunted as he shifted position.

21   "Strange place to spend your working day," I remarked.

22   "You're not wrong," he replied, sourly.

23   His older colleague seemed glad for a break. He stood, a portly man in a black tracksuit and fleece jacket, and stretched his back. Somehow he dimmed the light and the tomb settled back into restful gloom. The outside world was a square at the far end of the long passageway. There would be no sunset.

24   "Too bad," the surveyor said. "Oh, well."

25   Rob, hunched in his woolly hat, drew breath and raised his torch as though to begin the guided tour, but he paused.

26   "Been here before?" he asked me.

27   "Several times."

28   He said, "We're on the Web now, y'know," and gestured with the torch to a camera mounted on the Neolithic wall. "Live. Don't go picking your nose."

29   "Watch your eyes!" said the voice from the grave-chamber, then came a detonating flash.

[END OF PASSAGE]

FOR OFFICIAL USE

C

Total Mark

0860/406

NATIONAL QUALIFICATIONS 2007

TUESDAY, 1 MAY
2.30 PM – 3.20 PM

ENGLISH
STANDARD GRADE
Credit Level
Reading
Questions

Fill in these boxes and read what is printed below.

Full name of centre

MADRAS COLLEGE

Town

ST ANDREWS

Forename(s)

CAITLIN

Surname

ROTTGER

Date of birth
Day Month Year

0 7 0 7 9 4

Scottish candidate number

Number of seat

NB Before leaving the examination room you must give this booklet to the invigilator. If you do not, you may lose all the marks for this paper.

SCOTTISH
QUALIFICATIONS
AUTHORITY

©

Marks

QUESTIONS

Write your answers in the spaces provided.

Look at Paragraphs 1 and 2.

1. Give the meaning of "interred" and show how the context helped you to arrive at that meaning.

   Meaning: _____

   Context: _____   2 | 1 | 0

2. Write down **two** examples of the writer's use of **contrast** from Paragraph 1.

   _____

   _____   2 | 1 | 0

3. "a thin isthmus" (Paragraph 2)

   Tick the box beside the best definition of "isthmus".

area of land	
strip of land with water on each side	
stretch of moorland	
bridge connecting two islands	

   2 | ■ | 0

4. Identify the figure of speech used by the writer to describe the Standing Stones of Stenness. What does it suggest about the stones?

   _____

   _____   2 | 1 | 0

5. **In your own words**, explain what the writer finds to "marvel at" in the village of Skara Brae.

   _____

   _____   2 | 1 | 0

PAGE
TOTAL

Marks

6. What do you think the writer means when she says Skara Brae "re-calibrates your sense of time"?

_____

_____   2 1 0

Look at Paragraphs 3 to 8.

7. Why do you think the writer uses "improbable" to describe the older man's tartan trousers?

_____   2 ■ 0

8. Why does the man shake his head sadly as the writer steps out of her car?

_____   2 ■ 0

Look at Paragraphs 9 to 14.

9. Give **three** pieces of evidence which suggest that Maes Howe is just like any other tourist attraction.

_____

_____

_____   2 1 0

10. In your own words, give **two** reasons why the writer cannot buy a ticket in advance for the solstice.

_____

_____   2 1 0

[Turn over

[0860/406]   *Page three*

PAGE
TOTAL

Marks

11. Comment on the writer's use of word choice **and** sentence structure in her description of the clouds in the final sentence of Paragraph 14.

    (*a*) Word choice:

    _____

    _____   2 1 0

    (*b*) Sentence structure:

    _____

    _____   2 1 0

Look at Paragraphs 15 and 16.

12. In what way is entry to the inner chamber "more of a journey than a gateway"?

    _____   2 ■ 0

13. **In your own words**, describe **two** sensations which might be felt by someone entering the cairn.

    _____

    _____   2 1 0

14. What does a visitor notice and feel about the builders of Maes Howe? **Answer in your own words**.

    _____

    _____   2 1 0

15. (*a*) What style does the writer adopt in Paragraphs 15 and 16?

    _____   2 ■ 0

    (*b*) Support your answer with **two** pieces of evidence.

    _____   2 1 0

PAGE
TOTAL

Marks

Look at Paragraph 17.

16. Why did the builders of Maes Howe position it as they did?

_____

_____   2 | 1 | 0

17. What does the use of the word "apparently" tell you about the writer's attitude to the idea that some people find the experience in the tomb "overwhelming"?

_____   2 | ■ | 0

Look at Paragraphs 18 and 19.

18. Why was the inside of the tomb "as bright as a tube train"?

_____   2 | 1 | 0

19. Why do you think the writer includes the **comparison** of looking at her mother at the end of Paragraph 19?

_____

_____   2 | 1 | 0

[Turn over for Questions 20 to 23 on *Page six*

PAGE
TOTAL

Marks

Look at Paragraphs 20 to 28.

20. What evidence is there that the surveyors are doing a **thorough** job inside Maes Howe?

_____

_____   2 | 1 | 0

21. Give a possible reason for the surveyor answering the writer "sourly".

_____   2 | ■ | 0

22. In what way has Maes Howe become more accessible?

_____   2 | 1 | 0

Think about the passage as a whole.

23. Why might "Darkness and Light" be considered an appropriate title for this passage?

_____

_____   2 | 1 | 0

[END OF QUESTION PAPER]

PAGE TOTAL

[BLANK PAGE]

G

0860/403

NATIONAL
QUALIFICATIONS
2008

TUESDAY, 6 MAY
1.00 PM – 1.50 PM

ENGLISH
STANDARD GRADE
General Level
Reading
Text

Read carefully the passage overleaf. It will help if you read it twice. When you have done so, answer the questions. Use the spaces provided in the Question/Answer booklet.

Saddle the white horses

Thurso prepares to host its first professional surf tour, confirming Scotland's status as a world–class surfing destination.

1 It was the stickers that gave it away. Turning left on the A9 at Latheron in Caithness, you were suddenly faced with a sign that looked as though it had been defaced by advertising executives from surfing companies. Like a cairn on a mountain path, the big green board declaring Thurso to be 23 miles away told travelling bands of surfers that they'd taken the right turn-off and were nearly at their destination. Slapping another sticker on the sign was like laying another stone on the pile.

2 Thurso is about to enter surfing's big league.

3 It's hard to reconcile the popular tropical imagery of surfing with the town, a raw, exposed kind of place that enjoys little escape from the worst excesses of the Scottish climate. The Caithness coastline is peppered with surfing spots, but the jewel in the crown and the target for dedicated wave riders lies within spitting distance of Thurso town centre at a reef break called Thurso East. In the right conditions, the swell there rears up over kelp-covered slabs into a fast-moving, barrelling monster of a wave considered world class by those in the know.

4 Now Thurso East is the focus of a huge professional surfing tour. The week-long Highland Open marks the first time a World Qualifying Series (WQS) surfing competition has been held in Scotland. It will also be the furthest north a WQS tour has ever travelled, anywhere in the world.

5 Professional competitive surfing has two tours: the WQS and the World Championship Tour (WCT). The WCT is the premier division, with the WQS being used as a platform for professionals to move up into the big time. Around 160 up-and-coming wave riders are expected to take part in the Thurso event. Prize money of $100,000 (£57,000) is up for grabs, along with vital tour points.

6 "Travelling and exploring new places is part of the whole surfing culture," says Bernhard Ritzer, the Highland Open event manager. "We've had so much feedback from surfers from Australia and Brazil who want to go. They see it as an adventure and as something new. We did a photo trip there last year with some of our team riders and they were impressed. They're excited about it—although it will still be a shock because I don't think they know how cold and harsh it can be."

7 "Thurso is one of the best waves in Europe, if not the world," he says. "Most people don't even know it, and it's just so good. It doesn't always have to be sunny, warm and tropical. It can also be cold, rough and hard.

8 "The idea is to have a contrast to the summer events in the tropical islands. We also have something in the north to show that this is part of surfing. Very often on the WQS tour the waves aren't that good, but here they are expecting big reef break waves and they like to surf those."

9 Surfers generally guard their local breaks jealously. It's considered essential to keep your mouth shut about your "secret spot", in case you find it overrun with visitors. So, economic benefits to Thurso aside, some local surfers were a little concerned about an event on this scale descending on their area. WQS representatives met with these surfers to address their concerns and feel that they've pretty much got everyone on board. WQS is also paying for improvements to the car parking area near the Thurso East break.

10 "We're concerned to get the locals involved," says Ritzer. "We want to keep them happy and don't want to look too commercial, coming in with a big event machine. We need them to help organise local stuff. You always have some individuals who will boycott everything, but we understand that most of them are positive."

14   Robertson, 23, who has been surfing since he was four, criss-crosses the globe with his fellow WQS competitors in pursuit of the best waves and a place on the coveted WCT tour. He may as well be going to surf on the moon for all he knows about Thurso East, but that's part of the appeal.

15   "We follow the surf around all year and go to a lot of different places, but Scotland's somewhere probably none of us have been to," he says. "That for me was a big part of wanting to go, to see the place. As a professional surfer, you've got to live out of your bag a lot, travelling around with long stints away from home, but when you perform well in the event or get some really good waves, it makes it all worth it.

16   "I feel pretty good and I'm hoping to do well," he adds. "Everyone who does the tour is feeling good too, so it should be a great event. It'll be interesting to see what the waves are like."

17   Competitors will be scored by a team of eight international judges on the length of their ride, the difficulty of moves and how they connect it all together. Waves are scored on a one to ten scale, with ten a perfect ride, and the final scores are based on each surfer's two highest-scoring waves.

18   "These events raise the profile of locations, create investment in areas and hopefully provide opportunities for young surfers coming through to grow and compete at world-class levels," says Dave Reed, contest director for the WQS event. "It's a great way to say we've got some of the best waves in the world."

Adapted from a magazine article

[END OF PASSAGE]

11   Andy Bain probably knows the break at Thurso East better than anyone, although he'll be watching the competition from the shoreline. Bain, who runs Thurso Surf, has been surfing the reef there for 17 years and is eagerly anticipating the arrival of the Highland Open. He's aware of the concerns and the possible exposure of his home break, but doesn't anticipate a negative impact.

12   "From the surf school side of things it's good because it'll generate business for us," says Bain, 33. "As a local surfer, it's kind of like closure for me to have this competition. To say the world has now recognised Thurso as a top surfing destination makes me feel proud. A lot of people say it's going to get crowded and exposed, but with it being a cold destination I don't think it's going to be that bad."

13   For professional surfer Adam Robertson from Victoria, Australia, the trip to Thurso will be something of a journey into the unknown. "This will be the first time I've ever been to Scotland," says Robertson, who has competed on the WQS tour for the past three years. "We're all a bit worried about how cold it's going to be. Apart from that we're pretty excited because it's a place we've never been."

[BLANK PAGE]

FOR OFFICIAL USE

G

Total Mark

0860/404

NATIONAL QUALIFICATIONS 2008

TUESDAY, 6 MAY 1.00 PM – 1.50 PM

ENGLISH
STANDARD GRADE
General Level
Reading
Questions

Fill in these boxes and read what is printed below.

Full name of centre

Town

Forename(s)

Surname

Date of birth
Day Month Year

Scottish candidate number

Number of seat

NB Before leaving the examination room you must give this booklet to the invigilator. If you do not, you may lose all the marks for this paper.

Marks

QUESTIONS

Write your answers in the spaces provided.

Look at Paragraphs 1 to 3.

1. (*a*)   What had been added to the road sign in Caithness?

   _____

   _____   2 ■ 0

   (*b*)   Write down **two** things the surfers would know when they saw this road sign.

   _____

   _____   2 1 0

2. "Thurso is about to enter surfing's big league." (Paragraph 2)

   How does the writer make this statement stand out?

   _____   2 ■ 0

3. Thurso is different from the popular image of a surfing location.

   (*a*)   **In your own words**, describe the popular image of a surfing location.

   _____   2 ■ 0

   (*b*)   **Write down an expression** showing how Thurso is different.

   _____   2 ■ 0

4. What do the words "jewel in the crown" (Paragraph 3) suggest about Thurso East?

   _____   2 ■ 0

5. ". . . a fast-moving, barrelling monster . . ." (Paragraph 3)

   Explain fully why this is an effective description of the wave.

   _____

   _____   2 1 0

PAGE
TOTAL

Marks

Look at Paragraphs 4 and 5.

6. In which **two** ways is the Highland Open different from other WQS surfing competitions?

    (i) _____

    (ii) _____   2 | 1 | 0

7. **In your own words**, explain the difference between the two professional surfing tours.

    WCT _____

    WQS _____   2 | 1 | 0

8. Which **two** benefits will the winner of the competition gain?

    (i) _____

    (ii) _____   2 | 1 | 0

Look at Paragraphs 6 to 8.

9. Give **three** reasons why, according to Bernhard Ritzer, surfers will want to visit Thurso.

    (i) _____

    (ii) _____

    (iii) _____   2 | 1 | 0

10. According to Ritzer, what will surprise the surfers?

    _____   2 | ■ | 0

[Turn over

PAGE
TOTAL

Marks

11. Thurso can offer something which many other surfing locations cannot.

What is this?

_____

2 ■ 0

Look at Paragraphs 9 and 10.

12. "Surfers generally guard their local breaks . . . " (Paragraph 9)

In your own words, explain why surfers do this.

_____

2 1 0

13. What **style** of language is used in the expression "keep your mouth shut" (Paragraph 9)?

_____

2 ■ 0

14. Which **two key** things have WQS representatives done to gain support?

(i) _____

(ii) _____

2 1 0

15. The WQS representatives feel that "they've pretty much got everyone on board." (Paragraph 9)

Write down an expression from Paragraph 10 which continues this idea.

_____

2 ■ 0

16. Write down a single word from this section meaning "refuse to support or take part".

2 ■ 0

PAGE TOTAL

Marks

Look at Paragraphs 11 to 18.

17. (*a*) How does local surfer Andy Bain feel about the competition?

Tick (✓) the best answer.

very negative and angry	
quite pleased but worried	
excited and not really anxious	

2 ■ 0

(*b*) **Write down an expression** to support your chosen answer.

_____

2 ■ 0

18. "He may as well be going to surf on the moon . . . " (Paragraph 14)

What does this comparison suggest about Thurso?

_____

2 ■ 0

19. In Paragraph 15, Australian Adam Robertson describes his life as a professional surfer.

In your own words, sum up the **negative** and **positive** aspects of his life.

(*a*) **negative:** _____

_____

2 1 0

(*b*) **positive:** _____

_____

2 1 0

20. What **three** elements of the surfers' performance are judged?

(i) _____

(ii) _____

(iii) _____

2 1 0

[Turn over

PAGE
TOTAL

Marks

Think about the passage as a whole.

21.   (i)   What do you think is the main purpose of this passage?

Tick (✓) **one** box.

to tell the reader some amusing stories about surfing	
to inform the reader about a surfing competition in Scotland	
to argue against holding a surfing competition in Scotland	

(ii)   Give a reason to support your answer.

_____

_____

2   1   0

[END OF QUESTION PAPER]

FOR OFFICIAL USE

p2	
p3	
p4	
p5	
p6	
TOTAL MARK	

[BLANK PAGE]

[BLANK PAGE]

Official SQA Past Papers: Credit English 2008

C

0860/405

NATIONAL
QUALIFICATIONS
2008

TUESDAY, 6 MAY
2.30 PM – 3.20 PM

ENGLISH
STANDARD GRADE
Credit Level
Reading
Text

Read carefully the passage overleaf. It will help if you read it twice. When you have done so, answer the questions. Use the spaces provided in the Question/Answer booklet.

This passage, taken from the opening chapter of a novel, introduces us to the character of Briony and her family.

1   The play—for which Briony had designed the posters, programmes and tickets, constructed the sales booth out of a folding screen tipped on its side, and lined the collection box in red crêpe paper—was written by her in a two-day tempest of composition, causing her to miss a breakfast and a lunch. When the preparations were complete, she had nothing to do but contemplate her finished draft and wait for the appearance of her cousins from the distant north. There would be time for only one day of rehearsal before her brother, Leon, arrived.

2   At some moments chilling, at others desperately sad, the play told a tale of the heart whose message, conveyed in a rhyming prologue, was that love which did not build a foundation on good sense was doomed. The reckless passion of the heroine, Arabella, for a wicked foreign count is punished by ill fortune when she contracts cholera during an impetuous dash towards a seaside town with her intended. Deserted by him and nearly everybody else, bed-bound in an attic, she discovers in herself a sense of humour. Fortune presents her a second chance in the form of an impoverished doctor—in fact, a prince in disguise who has elected to work among the needy. Healed by him, Arabella chooses wisely this time, and is rewarded by reconciliation with her family and a wedding with the medical prince on "a windy sunlit day in spring".

3   Mrs Tallis read the seven pages of *The Trials of Arabella* in her bedroom, at her dressing table, with the author's arm around her shoulder the whole while. Briony studied her mother's face for every trace of shifting emotion, and Emily Tallis obliged with looks of alarm, snickers of glee and, at the end, grateful smiles and wise, affirming nods. She took her daughter in her arms, onto her lap, and said that the play was "stupendous", and agreed instantly, murmuring into the girl's ear, that this word could be quoted on the poster which was to be on an easel in the entrance hall by the ticket booth.

4   Briony was hardly to know it then, but this was the project's highest point of fulfilment. Nothing came near it for satisfaction, all else was dreams and frustration. There were moments in the summer dusk after her light was out, burrowing in the delicious gloom of her canopy bed, when she made her heart thud with luminous, yearning fantasies, little playlets in themselves, every one of which featured Leon. In one, his big, good-natured face buckled in grief as Arabella sank in loneliness and despair. In another, there he was, cocktail in hand at some fashionable city bar, overheard boasting to a group of friends: Yes, my younger sister, Briony Tallis the writer, you must surely have heard of her. In a third he punched the air in exultation as the final curtain fell, although there was no curtain, there was no possibility of a curtain. Her play was not for her cousins, it was for her brother, to celebrate his return, provoke his admiration and guide him away from his careless succession of girlfriends, towards the right form of wife, the one who would persuade him to return to the countryside, the one who would sweetly request Briony's services as a bridesmaid.

5   She was one of those children possessed by a desire to have the world just so. Whereas her big sister's room was a stew of unclosed books, unfolded clothes, unmade bed, unemptied ashtrays, Briony's was a shrine to her controlling demon: the model farm spread across a deep window ledge consisted of the usual animals, but all facing one way—towards their owner—as if about to break into song, and even the farmyard hens were neatly corralled. In fact, Briony's was the only tidy upstairs

room in the house. Her straight-backed dolls in their many-roomed mansion appeared to be under strict instructions not to touch the walls; the various thumb-sized figures to be found standing about her dressing table—cowboys, deep-sea divers, humanoid mice—suggested by their even ranks and spacing a citizen army awaiting orders.

6   A taste for the miniature was one aspect of an orderly spirit. Another was a passion for secrets: in a prized varnished cabinet, a secret drawer was opened by pushing against the grain of a cleverly turned dovetail joint, and here she kept a diary locked by a clasp, and a notebook written in a code of her own invention. In a toy safe opened by six secret numbers she stored letters and postcards. An old tin petty cash box was hidden under a removable floorboard beneath her bed. In the box were treasures that dated back four years, to her ninth birthday when she began collecting: a mutant double acorn, fool's gold, a rain-making spell bought at a funfair, a squirrel's skull as light as a leaf.

7   At the age of eleven she wrote her first story—a foolish affair, imitative of half a dozen folk tales and lacking, she realised later, that vital knowingness about the ways of the world which compels a reader's respect. But this first clumsy attempt showed her that the imagination itself was a source of secrets: once she had begun a story, no one could be told. Pretending in words was too tentative, too vulnerable, too embarrassing to let anyone know. Even writing out the *she saids*, the *and thens*, made her wince, and she felt foolish, appearing to know about the emotions of an imaginary being. Self-exposure was inevitable the moment she described a character's weakness; the reader was bound to speculate that she was describing herself. What other authority could she have? Only when a story was finished could she feel immune, and ready to punch holes in the margins, bind the chapters with pieces of string, paint or draw the cover, and take the finished work to show to her mother, or her father, when he was home.

8   Her efforts received encouragement. In fact, they were welcomed as the Tallises began to understand that the baby of the family possessed a strange mind and a facility with words. Briony was encouraged to read her stories aloud in the library and it surprised her parents and older sister to hear their quiet girl perform so boldly, making big gestures with her free arm, arching her eyebrows as she did the voices, and looking up from the page for seconds at a time as she read in order to gaze into one face after the other, unapologetically demanding her family's total attention as she cast her narrative spell.

9   The play she had written for Leon's homecoming was her first attempt at drama, and she had found the change quite effortless. It was a relief not to be writing out the *she saids*, or describing the weather or the onset of spring or her heroine's face—beauty, she had discovered, occupied a narrow band. Ugliness, on the other hand, had infinite variation. *The Trials of Arabella* was intended to inspire not laughter, but terror, relief and instruction, in that order, and the innocent intensity with which Briony set about the project—the posters, tickets, sales booth—made her particularly vulnerable to failure.

[END OF PASSAGE]

[BLANK PAGE]

FOR OFFICIAL USE

C

72%

Total Mark 36

0860/406

NATIONAL
QUALIFICATIONS
2008

TUESDAY, 6 MAY
2.30 PM – 3.20 PM

ENGLISH
STANDARD GRADE
Credit Level
Reading
Questions

Fill in these boxes and read what is printed below.

Full name of centre

MADRAS COLLEGE

Town

ST. ANDREWS

Forename(s)

CAITLIN

Surname

ROTTGER

Date of birth
Day Month Year

0 7 0 7 9 4

Scottish candidate number

Number of seat

**NB Before leaving the examination room you must give this booklet to the invigilator.
If you do not, you may lose all the marks for this paper.**

QUESTIONS

Write your answers in the spaces provided.

Marks

Look at Paragraph 1.

1. What task has Briony been involved in?

   ~~She~~ wrote ~~was~~ ~~writing~~ a play   ② ■ 0

2. In Paragraph 1, the writer shows how committed Briony has been to this task.

   Explain how **sentence structure** and **word choice** indicate Briony's high level of commitment.

   (*a*) **sentence structure:**

   The writer made a long list of things
   she ~~was~~ did connected to the plays   ② 1 0

   (*b*) **word choice:**

   ~~She had designed~~ "Briony had designed" and
   She "constructed" Suggests that she did it by
   herself and that she had bothered to "design" and
   construct things"   2 1 ⓪

Look at Paragraph 2.

3. Briony's play is a story with a message.

   In your own words, explain what the message is.

   out
   That love that ~~i~~ hasn't been sensibly thought ~~of~~
   ~~is~~ is ~~xxx~~ not going to work out   ② 1 0

6

PAGE
TOTAL

Marks

4. Read the writer's description of Briony's play in Paragraph 2, beginning: "The reckless passion of the heroine . . ."

   (*a*) What seems to be the writer's attitude to Briony's play?

   Thinks it's going to be dramatic

   2 1 ⓪

   (*b*) Quote **one** detail from the description and explain how it conveys this attitude.

   2 1 ⓪

Look at Paragraph 3.

5. ". . . and Emily Tallis obliged . . ." (Paragraph 3)

   What does the word "**obliged**" suggest about Emily's reaction to the play?

   That she thought it was dramatic and very good

   2 ▪ ⓪

6. Give **two** ways in which the writer emphasises the closeness between Briony and her mother.

   (i) *That Briony ~~and her~~ had her arm round her mom the whole way through*

   (ii) *The word choice of "Stupendous" suggests that her mum encourages her and please her*

   ② 1 0

Look at Paragraphs 4 and 5.

7. We are told that Briony's imagination took over "after her light was out". (Paragraph 4)

   By **referring closely** to the passage, **explain** how the writer's word choice indicates the **intensity** of Briony's fantasies.

   "luminous, yearning fantacies" ~~yes the~~ word "yearning"

   ~~suggests~~ ←are strong words and the word "thud" ~~▪~~ are

   wh

   2 1 ⓪

   [Turn over

2

PAGE
TOTAL

Marks

8. How does Briony want her brother, Leon, to **feel** about her writing?

   Quote an expression from the passage to support your answer.

   Wants him to feel proud of her writing and her "provoke his admiration"

   2 1 0

9. Look closely at the **final sentence** of Paragraph 4.

   In your own words, give **two** reasons why Briony has written the play for her brother.

   She wants him to find the perfect, sensible person for him to marry and for that girl to encourage him to come back to the country

   2 1 0

10. In Paragraph 5, the writer develops a **contrast** between Briony and her big sister.

    (a) **In your own words**, state what the contrast is.

    Person

    That Briony is a very neat and tidy but her sister leaves things lying around an untidy person

    2 1 0

    (b) By referring to **sentence structure** and **word choice**, explain how this contrast is developed.

    You should refer to **both** characters in **both** parts of your answer.

    (i) **sentence structure:** The In both

    By developing a list of things her sisters room is like compared to the list of what Briony's room is like.

    2 1 0

    (ii) **word choice:** By using the opposites of words "unfolded" especially "unopened" as opposed to closed to fit in with the rest of the words "unfolded" and "unmade" to talk about the sisters, room. Compared to the "Shrine" to describe Briony's room as though she treats it like her temple.

    2 1 0

9

PAGE
TOTAL

Marks

11. Explain the function of the **dashes** in the expression "— towards their owner—". (Paragraph 5)

Because it's added information but the sentence would make sense without it.

② 1 0

Look at Paragraph 6.

12. "Another was a passion for secrets:" (Paragraph 6)

By referring to the passage, show how the writer continues this idea in the rest of the paragraph.

By going on to talk about all of Briony's secret things or places and

② 1 0

13. Explain why a **colon** is used in the expression "when she began collecting:" (Paragraph 6)

To then go Because the writer a list of things she collected followed that sentence

② 1 0

14. What do the items in Briony's collection suggest about her as a person?

That she is an unusual girl who likes collecting unusual things

② ■ 0

Look at Paragraph 7.

15. Briony wrote her first story when she was eleven.

In your own words, give **two** reasons why she later disliked this story.

(i) Because that it was basically copy 6 fairy stories

(ii) Because she didn't know much about life then

② 1 0

16. Explain **in your own words** why Briony was concerned about describing a character's weakness.

Because she thought her as people that read the book would assume the description was based on her

② 1 0

[Turn over for Questions 17 to 20 on *Page six*

11

PAGE TOTAL

Marks

17. Quote one word from Paragraph 7 showing that Briony was no longer vulnerable when the story was finished.

"immune"

2 ■ 0

Look at Paragraphs 8 and 9.

18. Explain why Briony's performance in the library surprised her family.

Answer in your own words.

Because she is normally a shy girl but when she was reading she was very confident

2 1 0

19. Why did Briony prefer writing about **ugly** rather than **beautiful** characters?

Use your own words in your explanation.

Because there is only a few forms of beauty but ugliness there are loads more descriptions she could make

2 1 0

Think about the passage as a whole.

20. In Briony, the writer has created a character who is both **imaginative** and **anxious**.

By referring closely to the passage, show how both these aspects of her personality have been conveyed to the reader.

(i) **imaginative:**

They have been conveyed by her writing about of the imaginative stories and her imaginative hiding places

2 1 0

(ii) **anxious:**

By her nervousness during writing the books and her dislike of what she is writing because it seems she is opening up.

2 1 0

[END OF QUESTION PAPER]

8

PAGE
TOTAL

[BLANK PAGE]

F
G
C

0860/407

NATIONAL
QUALIFICATIONS
2006

WEDNESDAY, 3 MAY
9.00 AM – 10.15 AM

ENGLISH
STANDARD GRADE
Foundation, General
and Credit Levels
Writing

Read This First

1 Inside this booklet, there are photographs and words.
   Use them to help you when you are thinking about what to write.
   Look at all the material and think about all the possibilities.

2 There are 21 assignments altogether for you to choose from.

3 Decide which assignment you are going to attempt.
   Choose only **one** and write its number in the margin of your answer book.

4 Pay close attention to what you are asked to write.
   Plan what you are going to write.
   Read and check your work before you hand it in.
   Any changes to your work should be made clearly.

SCOTTISH
QUALIFICATIONS
AUTHORITY

©

Page two

FIRST   **Look at the picture opposite.**
         It shows a couple parting.

NEXT   Think how you might feel about leaving someone you care for.

WHAT YOU HAVE TO WRITE

---

1. **Write about** a time when you were separated from someone you cared about.

   You should concentrate on your **thoughts and feelings**.

   OR

2. **Write a short story** using the title:

   Never Forgotten.

   OR

3. We should be less afraid to speak openly about our feelings.
   Discuss.

   OR

4. **Write in any way you choose** using the picture opposite as your inspiration.

                                                                    [Turn over

FIRST   **Look at the picture opposite.**
                It shows a lightning strike.

NEXT   Think about the power of storms.

WHAT YOU HAVE TO WRITE

---

5. **Describe** both the excitement and the fear you experienced when you were caught in a storm.

   OR

6. **Write a short story** using **ONE** of the following titles:
   Stormchaser   Lightning Strikes Twice.

   OR

7. **Write a newspaper article** with the following headline:
   Storm Causes Widespread Damage.

   OR

8. Weather plays an important part in our everyday lives.
   Give your views.

[Turn over

FIRST   **Look at the picture opposite.**
        It shows a group of students.

NEXT   Think about life during and after school.

| WHAT YOU HAVE TO WRITE |

9. **Giving reasons**, write about your plans for when you leave school.

    OR

10. **Write a short story** using the following title:

    The Examination.

    OR

11. **Write an article** for your school magazine in which you describe the high points **and** the low points of your school years.

    OR

12. New places, new faces.

    Write about a time when you had to cope with new people in new surroundings.

    Remember to include your **thoughts and feelings**.

                                                                [Turn over

FIRST   **Look at the picture opposite.**
         It shows a traffic jam.

NEXT   Think about travel problems.

WHAT YOU HAVE TO WRITE

---

13. **Write about** an occasion when you were delayed during a journey.
    You should concentrate on your **thoughts and feelings**.

    OR

14. **Write a short story** using the following title:
    The Road to Nowhere.

    OR

15. Road rage, air rage—the modern age.
    Life today is simply too stressful.
    Discuss.

                                                              [Turn over

FIRST   **Look at the picture opposite.**
             It shows a young couple who have fallen out.

NEXT   Think about relationships.

WHAT YOU HAVE TO WRITE

16. **Write a short story** using **ONE** of the following openings:

    EITHER

    Jill stared ahead intently, always away from him, focused firmly on
    the wall. He tried to speak. She raised her arm in protest . . .

    OR

    Andrew didn't know what to do. Just hours earlier things had
    been simply perfect. Now this. He let his mind wander back to . . .

    OR

17. Magazines for young people do more good than harm.
    Give your views.

    OR

18. **Write about** your **thoughts and feelings** at a time when you
    were aware that someone simply wasn't listening.

[Turn over for assignments 19 to 21 on *Page twelve*

There are no pictures for these assignments.

19. **Write a short story** using the following opening.

    "He awoke in the ashes of a dead city. The cruel sun glared, showing neither pity nor mercy. He shook himself. It was no dream."

    Make sure that you develop **character** and **setting** as well as **plot**.

    OR

20. Look at me!

    Is it more important to be an individual or to fit in with the crowd?

    Discuss.

    OR

21. **Write a short story** using the title:

    Out of Time.

    Make sure that you develop **character** and **setting** as well as **plot**.

[END OF QUESTION PAPER]

2007 Writing | Foundation | General | Credit

[BLANK PAGE]

F
G
C

0860/407

NATIONAL
QUALIFICATIONS
2007

TUESDAY, 1 MAY
9.00 AM – 10.15 AM

ENGLISH
STANDARD GRADE
Foundation, General
and Credit Levels
Writing

Read This First

1   Inside this booklet, there are photographs and words.
    Use them to help you when you are thinking about what to write.
    Look at all the material and think about all the possibilities.

2   There are 23 assignments altogether for you to choose from.

3   Decide which assignment you are going to attempt.
    Choose only **one** and write its number in the margin of your answer book.

4   Pay close attention to what you are asked to write.
    Plan what you are going to write.
    Read and check your work before you hand it in.
    Any changes to your work should be made clearly.

SCOTTISH
QUALIFICATIONS
AUTHORITY

SA 0860/407 6/75170   ©

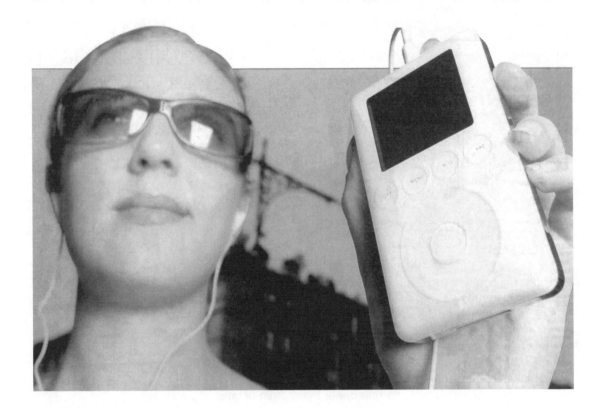

FIRST   **Look at the picture opposite.**
It shows a young woman with an MP3 player.

NEXT   Think about the importance of technology.

WHAT YOU HAVE TO WRITE

---

1. The one piece of technology I couldn't live without.
   Write about the importance to you of **ONE** piece of technology.

   OR

2. Young people today care too much for personal possessions.
   Give your views.

   OR

3. **Write a short story** using **ONE** of the following titles:
   Futureshock   She Saw the Future.
   You should develop **setting** and **character** as well as **plot**.

[Turn over

FIRST   **Look at the picture opposite.**
         It shows a young boy being led by his mother.

NEXT   Think about your schooldays.

WHAT YOU HAVE TO WRITE

4. School Memories.

   Write about a person, place, or incident from your schooldays which you find unforgettable.

   Remember to include your **thoughts and feelings**.

   OR

5. **Write a short story** using the following opening:

   The reluctance was written all over John's face. He tugged at his mother's hand. He winced. He grimaced. He complained. Still his mother led him on . . .

   You should develop **setting** and **character** as well as **plot**.

   OR

6. All pupils should wear school uniform.

   Give your views.

[Turn over

FIRST   **Look at the picture opposite.**
         It shows a lake in winter.

NEXT   Think about special places.

WHAT YOU HAVE TO WRITE

7. Sometimes a special place can inspire us.

   Write about such a place.

   Remember to include your **thoughts and feelings**.

   OR

8. **Write in any way you choose** using the picture opposite as your inspiration.

   OR

9. **Write about** a time when you were alone but happy.

   You should concentrate on your **thoughts and feelings**.

   OR

10. **Write an informative article** for a travel magazine titled:

    The Best Holiday Destination For Young People.

[Turn over

FIRST   **Look at the picture opposite.**
                  It shows a man under pressure.

NEXT   Think about the pressures of life.

WHAT YOU HAVE TO WRITE

11. **Write about** a time in your life when you had to face personal pressure.

   You should describe your **thoughts and feelings**.

   OR

12. **Write a short story** using **ONE** of the following titles:

   The Underdog   Free at Last.

   You should develop **setting** and **character** as well as **plot**.

   OR

13. It's Just Not Fair!

   Write about an occasion when you took a stand against injustice.

   You should concentrate on your **thoughts and feelings** as well as what you did.

   OR

14. These days young people are unfairly treated by the media.

   Give your views.

   [Turn over

FIRST   **Look at the picture opposite.**
         It shows a young woman on a bus, alone with her thoughts.

NEXT   Think about moments of reflection.

WHAT YOU HAVE TO WRITE

---

15. "The glass is always half full; never half empty."

    It is important to have a positive outlook on life.

    Give your views.

    OR

16. **Write about** an occasion when you had an unpleasant duty to perform.

    You should concentrate on your **thoughts and feelings**.

    OR

17. Act Your Age!

    There are fewer chances today simply to be yourself.

    Give your views.

    OR

18. **Write a short story** using **ONE** of the following titles:

    Stranger in a Strange Land   No Return.

    You should develop **setting** and **character** as well as **plot**.

    [Turn over for assignments 19 to 23 on *Page twelve*

There are no pictures for these assignments.

19. We should try to solve the problems here on earth before we spend more on space exploration.

    Give your views.

    OR

20. **Describe the scene** brought to mind by the following:

    A stark land of leafless trees and merciless wind.

    OR

21. We forget our past at our peril!

    Not enough is being done to keep Scottish heritage alive.

    Write a newspaper article in which you give your views on this topic.

    OR

22. There are special times of the year when people celebrate in their own way.

    Describe such a special time, bringing out its importance to you, your family, and your community.

    OR

23. **Write a short story** using the following title:

    The Traveller.

    You should develop **setting** and **character** as well as **plot**.

[END OF QUESTION PAPER]

[BLANK PAGE]

**F
G
C**

0860/407

NATIONAL
QUALIFICATIONS
2008

TUESDAY, 6 MAY
9.00 AM – 10.15 AM

ENGLISH
STANDARD GRADE
Foundation, General
and Credit Levels
Writing

Read This First

1   Inside this booklet, there are photographs and words.
    Use them to help you when you are thinking about what to write.
    Look at all the material and think about all the possibilities.

2   There are 22 assignments altogether for you to choose from.

3   Decide which assignment you are going to attempt.
    Choose only **one** and write its number in the margin of your answer book.

4   Pay close attention to what you are asked to write.
    Plan what you are going to write.
    Read and check your work before you hand it in.
    Any changes to your work should be made clearly.

FIRST   **Look at the picture opposite.**
         It shows a car in heavy rain and hail.

NEXT   Think about the dangers of extreme weather.

WHAT YOU HAVE TO WRITE

1. **Write a short story** using the following opening:

    The car skidded violently. He struggled to regain control. Close to panic, he wrenched the steering wheel to the right . . .

    You should develop **setting** and **character** as well as **plot**.

    OR

2. What's going on with our weather?

    Individuals need to take steps to tackle climate change.

    Give your views.

    OR

3. Journeys can take unexpected turns.

    Write about an occasion when this happened to **you**.

    Remember to include your **thoughts and feelings**.

                                                        [Turn over

FIRST   **Look at the picture opposite.**
It shows young people together in a school cafeteria.

NEXT   Think about school experiences.

WHAT YOU HAVE TO WRITE

4. A Best Friend Should Be . . .

    Write about the ideal qualities of a best friend.

    OR

5. Youth culture. There's no such thing.

    Give your views.

    OR

6. **Write about** an occasion when your loyalty to a friend was pushed to the limit.

    Remember to include your **thoughts and feelings**.

    OR

7. **Write a short story** using the following title:

    The School Gate.

    You should develop **setting** and **character** as well as **plot**.

[Turn over

FIRST **Look at the picture opposite.
It shows a man staring.**

NEXT Think about being observed.

WHAT YOU HAVE TO WRITE

8. Big Brother is Watching You!

   Write about an occasion when you felt that there was no escape from authority.

   Remember to include your **thoughts and feelings**.

   OR

9. **Write a short story** using **ONE** of the following titles:

   Seeing is Believing Close Up

   You should develop **setting** and **character** as well as **plot**.

   OR

10. All You Need is an Audience.

    The media give young people the idea that success comes easily.

    Give your views.

[Turn over

Page eight

FIRST   **Look at the picture opposite.
It shows a boy with his grandfather.**

NEXT   Think about the positive relationship you have with an older relative.

WHAT YOU HAVE TO WRITE

11. **Write about** an occasion when you learned a valuable lesson from an older relative.

    Remember to include your **thoughts and feelings**.

    OR

12. **Write a short story** using the following opening:

    Those were the moments he loved most. Grandpa reading to him with that lilting voice telling stories of . . .

    You should develop **setting** and **character** as well as **plot**.

    OR

13. We do not give the older generation the respect they deserve.

    Give your views.

    OR

14. **Write in any way you choose** using the picture opposite as your inspiration.

[Turn over

FIRST **Look at the picture opposite.
It shows an aircraft in the sunset.**

NEXT Think about air travel.

WHAT YOU HAVE TO WRITE

15. The damage to the environment caused by aircraft outweighs the advantages of cheap air travel.

   Give your views.

   OR

16. **Write a short story** using **ONE** of the following titles:

   A New Beginning   Touchdown

   You should develop **setting** and **character** as well as **plot**.

   OR

17. **Write in any way you choose** using the picture opposite as your inspiration.

   [Turn over for assignments 18 to 22 on *Page twelve*

There are no pictures for these assignments.

18. **Write an informative article** for your school magazine titled:

   Technology: the impact on my education.

   OR

19. Nowadays there is less freedom of choice.
   Give your views.

   OR

20. **Write a short story** with the following opening:

   Beth stared again at the square glow from the computer screen in disbelief. She was going to be reunited with her sister at long last. She could hardly wait . . .

   You should develop **setting** and **character** as well as **plot**.

   OR

21. Education is about what we learn both **inside** and **outside** the classroom.
   Give your views.

   OR

22. **Describe the scene** brought to mind by **ONE** of the following:
   EITHER

   Snow fell, the flimsiest drops of geometric perfection, lightly, gently onto the village rooftops.

   OR

   With merciless rage, the sun scorched the earth to brittle hardness.

[END OF QUESTION PAPER]

[BLANK PAGE]

[BLANK PAGE]

[BLANK PAGE]

[BLANK PAGE]

[BLANK PAGE]

Acknowledgements

Leckie and Leckie is grateful to the copyright holders, as credited, for permission to use their material:

The Mail on Sunday for the article 'Pucker way to kiss a hummingbird' by Mark Carwardine (2004 General Reading paper p 2);

The BBC for a photograph (2004 General Reading paper p 2);

Getty Images for a photograph (2004 Writing paper p 2);

Getty Images for a photograph (2004 Writing paper p 8);

Camera Press, London, for a photograph by John Swannell (2004 Writing paper p 10);

The Sunday Times for the article 'Dazzling the Stars' by John Harlow (2005 General Reading paper p 2);

Freefoto.com for a photograph (2005 Writing paper p 4);

The Scotsman for a photograph (2005 Writing paper p 6);

Ralph A. Clevenger/Corbis for a photograph, © Ralph A Clevenger/CORBIS (2005 Writing paper p 8);

Getty/Matthew Cavanaugh for the photograph '77th Scripps Howard Spelling Bee Enters Final Round' (2006 General Reading paper p 2);

The Scotsman for the photograph 'Scots will be squeezed out. Fee refugees!' (2006 Writing paper p 6);

Design Pics Inc./Alamy for the photograph 'People' (2006 Writing paper p 10);

The Sunday Telegraph for the article 'The Fabulous Biker Boys (and Girls)' by John Dodd (2007 Reading paper p 2);

Rex Features for a photograph 'iPod Generation' by Dan Callister (2007 Writing paper p 2); Getty Images for a photograph (2007 Writing paper p 4);

Dan Heller for a photograph from www.danheller.com (2007 Writing paper p 6);

Getty Images for a photograph by David Hogsholt (2007 Writing p 10);

An extract from 'Atonement' by Ian McEwan, published by Jonathan Cape. Reprinted by the permission of The Random House Group Ltd (2008 Reading paper pp 2-3);

Scotland on Sunday for a photograph 'Chips are down' by Robert Perry (2008 Writing Paper p 4);

FreeFoto.com for a photograph 'Airbus 320' by Ian Britton (2008 Writing Paper p 10).

The following companies have very generously given permission to reproduce their copyright material free of charge:

Captain Corelli's Mandolin by Louis de Berniéres, published by Martin Secker & Warburg. Reprinted by permission of The Random House Group. (2004 Credit Reading paper pp 2-3);

Maurice Lacroix Ltd for an advertisement (2004 Writing paper p 4); Newsquest Media Group for a photograph (2004 Writing paper p 4);

News Team International for a photograph (2004 Writing paper p 6);

Dark Star Safari: Overland from Cairo to Cape Town by Paul Theroux (Penguin Books 2002). Copyright © Cape Cod Scriveners Co. 2002.

Reproduced by permission of Penguin Books Ltd. (2005 Credit Reading paper pp 2-3);

Newsquest Media Group for a photograph 'High Hopes'(2005 Writing paper p 10);

TES Scotland for a photograph (2005 Writing paper p 10);

Pearson Education for an extract from You Don't Know Me by David Klass (2006 Reading paper pp 2-4);

Newsquest Media Group for the photograph 'Stretching the Nerves' by Kieran Dodds (2006 Writing paper p 8);

Steve Double for a picture 'Eye Opener' (2008 Writing Paper p 6);

Bigfoto.com for a picture (2008 Writing Paper p 2) .